Using Internet Primary Sources to Teach Critical Thinking Skills in Geography

Recent Titles in
Greenwood Professional Guides in School Librarianship

100 Research Topic Guides for Students
Barbara Wood Borne

Special Events Programs in School Library Media Centers: A Guide to Making
Them Work
Marcia Trotta

Information Services for Secondary Schools
Dana McDougald and Melvin Bowie

The Internet and the School Library Media Specialist: Transforming Traditional
Services
Randall M. MacDonald

Creating a Local Area Network in the School Library Media Center
Becky R. Mather

Collection Assessment and Management for School Libraries: Preparing for
Cooperative Collection Development
Debra E. Kachel

Using Educational Technology with At-Risk Students: A Guide for Library
Media Specialists and Teachers
Roxanne Baxter Mendrinos

Teaching Electronic Literacy: A Concepts-Based Approach for School Library
Media Specialists
Kathleen W. Craver

Block Scheduling and Its Impact on the School Library Media Center
Marie Keen Shaw

Using Internet Primary Sources to Teach Critical Thinking Skills in History
Kathleen W. Craver

100 More Research Topic Guides for Students
Dana McDougald

Curriculum Partner: Redefining the Role of the Library Media Specialist
Carol A. Kearney

Using Internet Primary Sources to Teach Critical Thinking Skills in Geography

Martha B. Sharma
and Gary S. Elbow

Greenwood Professional Guides in School Librarianship
Harriet Selverstone, Series Adviser

GREENWOOD PRESS
Westport, Connecticut • London

Library of Congress Cataloging-in-Publication Data

Sharma, Martha B., 1945–
    Using internet primary sources to teach critical thinking skills in geography /
    Martha B. Sharma and Gary S. Elbow.
        p. cm.—(Greenwood professional guides in school librarianship, ISSN 1074–150X)
    Includes bibliographical references (p.   ) and index.
        ISBN 0–313–30899–3 (alk. paper)
        1. Geography—Study and teaching (Secondary)—Computer network resources.   2.
    Internet in education.   3. Critical thinking—Study and teaching
    (Secondary) I. Elbow, Gary S. II. Title. III. Series.
    G73.S393   2000
    910'.285—dc21   99–088459

British Library Cataloguing in Publication Data is available.

Library of Congress Catalog Card Number: 99–088459
ISBN: 0–313–30899–3
ISSN: 1074–150X

First published in 2000

Greenwood Press, 88 Post Road West, Westport, CT 06881
An imprint of Greenwood Publishing Group, Inc.
www.greenwood.com

Printed in the United States of America

The paper used in this book complies with the
Permanent Paper Standard issued by the National
Information Standards Organization (Z39.48–1984).

10 9 8 7 6 5 4 3 2 1

Copyright Acknowledgments

The authors and publisher gratefully acknowledge permission to use the following material:

Excerpts from *Geography for Life: The National Geography Standards, 1994*, The Geography Education Standards Project, Washington, D.C. Copyright National Geographic Society. Reproduced with permission.

Contents

Acknowledgments

We wish to thank our respective institutions, National Cathedral School in Washington, D.C. and Texas Tech University in Lubbock, Texas, for the time, support, and access to facilities and resources that enabled us to undertake this project. We would also like to thank them for access to electronic mail, which made this long-distance collaboration possible. We appreciate the advice and encouragement of the editors at Greenwood Publishing, Debby Adams, Barbara Rader, and Harriet Selverstone, as well as the assistance of Production Editor Lynn Zelem and Copy Editor Arletta Anderson. Finally, we would like to thank our spouses, Naren and Margaret, for their patience and support throughout this venture into new territory for us both.

Martha B. Sharma and Gary S. Elbow

Introduction

Geography, as an area of study, is ideally suited to critical thinking. While often associated with memorization of isolated bits of information such as the names of capital cities, products of countries, or locations of ethnic groups, the real objective of geographical study is to be able to explain how places develop their special characteristics, why they are located where they are, and how they are related to each other. Taking a problem-centered approach helps students to learn better because they are able to generalize about where certain kinds of resources or activities may be located and they learn to associate certain patterns and processes. All of these activities require critical thinking skills.

In this book we provide ideas and resources that will help school librarians and teachers understand the discipline of geography and locate and use Internet sites that are especially useful in helping students develop critical thinking skills in the context of geography. However, it should be recognized from the outset that the same critical thinking skills are equally applicable to almost any other field of study. The element that sets each discipline apart is the kinds of questions it asks. Cultivating a geographic perspective involves being able to ask the proper kinds of questions and knowing where to obtain the information that is needed to be able to answer them.

The Internet or World Wide Web has emerged as a valuable new source from which to obtain the information needed to answer geographical questions. It is also sometimes possible to locate sites that provide specific kinds of exercises or modules to help students learn to apply critical thinking skills in geography, but such sites are much less common than more content-oriented sites. For this reason most of the sites we list here are content-oriented.

Chapter 1 examines the place of critical thinking in education and in geography education, specifically. It considers briefly the history of geography as an academic discipline and the evolution of geography education in the schools in the closing decades of the twentieth century. Because rote memorization of maps is so often mistaken for the study of geography, we have identified some central concepts and questions that define geography as an academic discipline that calls for regular use of critical thinking skills. Chapter 2 identifies and explains the types of sources upon which geographers rely, with special emphasis on primary sources. Chapter 3 provides a framework for undertaking research in geography. It links posing questions and hypotheses to the wide range of resources to which geographers turn as they seek answers. All but the most elemental levels of geographic research apply critical thinking skills in order to evaluate data and sources, and to translate information into knowledge. As different areas for research are defined, types of resources and examples of useful sites from the Internet are identified.

Chapter 4 provides background information and suggestions for using Internet resources to teach critical thinking in geography. The chapter is specifically directed to the needs of school librarians who are called upon by both teachers and students to locate and evaluate resources for teaching and learning; but teachers of geography, earth science, and social studies will also find this chapter useful. More and more, resources of geographic relevance may be found among the thousands of sites that appear on the Internet but this ever-expanding information storehouse requires a road map. It also requires some guidelines to help users identify particularly helpful sites and avoid those that have problems. For example, which sites have textual information, maps, or data that is of special value for geography students? Which sites are particularly oriented toward geography education? Since new sites are constantly being added to the Internet, users need to develop their own strategies to evaluate critically what they find there and determine for themselves to what extent a site presents useful information versus information that may contain inaccuracies or promote a particular agenda or point of view on the topic at hand. In Chapter 4 we have included an annotated list of sample Internet sites with questions and suggestions for their use in teaching critical thinking skills in a geographic context. This list requires two cautionary notes. First, the list represents only a sample of sites available; it is not all-inclusive and users should view it as a starting point, a list to which they will add other sites that they find useful. Second, the Internet, like geography, is dynamic—it is constantly changing. While every attempt has been made to include sites that are stable and likely to remain available, some sites may move, change addresses, or vanish altogether. Chapter 4 concludes with a brief list of resources to aid librarians and teachers in locating additional geography resources and in developing a program of geography instruction based on the critical use of resources from the Internet.

As suggested above, our basic premise is that the Internet can be a valuable teaching resource, but it is very much a two-edged sword which has the potential to misinform users as much as it informs them. Separating the Internet gems from the colored glass requires a high level of critical thinking skill, but by the same measure, the Internet itself, properly used, can be a useful tool for helping students to hone their critical thinking skills. We hope this book will serve as a guide to some of these resources and also provide some useful suggestions on how they may be used to teach critical thinking through geography.

Critical Thinking in Geography

1

The "information superhighway" has opened knowledge frontiers to more people than ever before. Access is without limits—no minimum age requirements, no maximum speed limits. The Internet opens the door to information on virtually any topic one might choose to investigate and it has the capability of presenting that information in a format which combines print, visual images, and sound. Having ready access to such a wide range of information in multiple formats and at little or no expense opens up learning opportunities that have never before existed.

Potentially, the Internet is the greatest learning tool since the invention of printing. Students can learn at their own pace, they can follow their own interests in choosing what topics to learn about, and they can acquire information through several different formats. With respect to critical thinking, the Internet not only provides a wonderful opportunity to develop habits of questioning, evaluation, and assessment; it demands such skills. Students have information choices unlike those of previous generations, but individuals or groups generating information have a largely unregulated outlet for posting data, opinions, and interpretations that may reflect a narrowly held point of view or promote the agenda of fringe political groups, religious sects, or conspiracy theorists, for example. Unlike most books and journals whose publishers usually subject content to close scrutiny and peer review, and which are further subject to evaluation by librarians, information appearing on the Internet is largely unfiltered. There is no review board to measure the validity of information posted on an expanding galaxy of home pages, nor is there a library acquisition process. Anyone with a computer and the right software can post information free of charge. This freedom of access to the

Internet is a tremendous asset for information exchange, but it also places a large burden on the user, who must take care to evaluate the quality of the material that she or he accesses. Thus, the Internet may be used to teach critical thinking practices in a context in which the need for such skills rapidly becomes evident.

WHAT IS CRITICAL THINKING?

Some years ago author Dorothy Sayers commented, " . . . although we often succeed in teaching our pupils 'subjects,' we fail lamentably on the whole in teaching them how to think: they learn everything except the art of learning" (Sayers 1979: 91). Sayers' concern rings true two decades later: Are we teaching our students to think—to question the flood of information before them, to examine issues for opposing points of view, to weigh arguments against tested criteria? In other words, are we equipping our students with the skills and habits of *critical thinking*?

Critical thinking is more than applying simple thought to a topic or issue; it is disciplined, reflective thinking. Critical thinking directs the habits of mind particular to a discipline, such as geography, to the issue or problem at hand, raising questions and using evidence in ways that reflect the perspectives of the discipline or domain that defines the issue.

Historically, one must look as far back as the early Greeks to trace the earliest recorded roots of critical thinking. Socrates, in his emphasis on the importance of questioning, laid the foundation for inquiry-based learning. He stressed the importance of arguments supported by evidence and careful reasoning. This approach to knowledge has defined the work of major thinkers since and underpins the scientific method. Questioning is the cornerstone of critical thinking which in turn is the source of knowledge formation and as such should be taught as a framework for all learning.

Students are frequently conditioned in their approach to learning by experiences in teacher-centered, textbook-driven classrooms. "Traditional textbooks are fact- rather than process-oriented. They stress 'what' instead of 'how' and 'why.' . . . when teachers allow textbooks to dominate instruction they are unlikely to meet today's educational demands for critical thinking, problem-solving, skill-building, and inquiry about the real world" (Hill 1994: 38–39). Such experiences contribute to a belief that answers are either right or wrong, textbooks are always right, and knowledge, as defined by the teacher and the textbook, is complete. Such an approach to learning is likely to leave students with a sense of powerlessness and an inclination to confuse learning with memorization of facts. It may foster an attitude that topics addressed in the classroom have little or nothing to do with the real world since classroom "facts" appear static while the real world is clearly dynamic. But more importantly, this approach to learning leaves students ill-equipped to deal with new and sometimes contradictory information. Students must be taught and encouraged to question.

Critical thinking is important for a number of reasons. It makes the learning process more meaningful and ultimately more rewarding because students become active rather than passive participants. It prepares the learner for effective participation in the workplace because it involves evaluation of an issue or problem from multiple perspectives and therefore supports reasoned decision-making. Likewise, critical thinking contributes to responsible citizenship because it fosters an analytical approach to issues of public concern and ballot choices.

Critical thinking is not an automatic response; it is a skill that must be taught, nurtured, and encouraged in the classroom. It requires a cultivated and purposeful unwillingness to accept information at face value. Students must be pushed beyond the passive comfort zone of absorbing what they read or hear and challenged to think, reason, question, and evaluate information presented. With reference to an issue or problem they need to begin to ask:

- What is the issue or argument?
- What evidence supports this position?
- What is the source of this evidence?
- Is this issue presented accurately? . . . completely?
- What assumptions have been made?
- Whose viewpoint is represented?
- Are there other ways of looking at this issue?
- What do I believe and why do I believe it?

Development of critical thinking skills requires not only practice and encouragement, but also a safe environment in which questioning is not regarded as a challenge to authority; in which knowledge is not viewed as absolute, but rather as dynamic and ever-evolving; in which there is room for more than one "right" answer. Most importantly, students need an environment in which to experiment with ideas, to test different points of view, and even to make mistakes without fear of censure. Critical thinking does not, however, mean wild speculation or undisciplined questioning. High intellectual standards must be set against which good questioning and evaluation can be measured. Creating a balanced environment—high standards coupled with freedom to test ideas—is one of the greatest challenges for educators.

Critical thinking does not occur in isolation; it occurs in association with an issue, argument, or problem. The questions raised necessarily reflect the context or perspectives of the discipline—be it science or math, history or geography—that provides the framework within which the issue is presented. Therefore, questions can be expected to vary among disciplines. Critical thinking presumes a basic understanding of the perspectives and concepts of the discipline in order to frame good questions. Geography is a discipline that lends itself especially well to the teaching and practice of critical thinking skills because of the volume and diversity of information with which it deals. Geographers are concerned with the physical and social character of countries and regions, with environmental issues, and with various aspects of location. Critical thinking is essential to understand, evaluate, and interrelate such information.

WHAT IS GEOGRAPHY?

Geography is one of the world's oldest disciplines, but for many people today, one of the least understood. The earliest practitioners of geography were Greek writers and philosophers who observed the world around them and tried to explain it. The oldest preserved effort to describe the world and explain differences among culture groups is attributed to the Greek writer, Herodotus, who lived in the sixth century B.C. He believed that cultures adopted characteristics that reflected the environments in which they lived. Herodotus' theory would not be accepted today, but the question he asked, "How do humans and environment interact?" is still one of the principal research questions of geography. The first use of the word "geography" followed Herodotus by 300 years and is attributed to the Greek philosopher Eratosthenes, who is best remembered for having devised an accurate means for determining the circumference of Earth. Strabo and Ptolemy, Greek philosophers living in the Roman Empire, wrote lengthy works, *Geography* and *Guide to Geography*, respectively, in an attempt to describe and explain both the physical and human phenomena of their world. The Romans valued the work of these and other early geographers as they worked to expand and control their vast empire. After the destruction of the library of Alexandria in A.D. 391, the works of Strabo and Ptolemy were largely forgotten in Europe. However, they were preserved by Arab scholars. Reintroduced to Europe during the Renaissance, they were consulted by Columbus and other explorers of the Age of Discovery.

During the Middle Ages interest in geography waned in an isolationist Europe, but thrived among Chinese and Islamic scholars, who represented more enlightened and expansionist cultures. In Europe the Crusades drew attention to alien lands, but attempts to find an empirical explanation for physical and cultural diversity were still far in the future. The work of early Renaissance travelers such as Marco Polo stimulated interest in largely descriptive geography but their tendency to mix fact with fable contributed relatively little to Western knowledge of the world. Fantastic as they were, these medieval travel accounts, along with the newly resurrected work of the Classical Roman geographers, provided the knowledge on which the Age of Exploration was based. Henry the Navigator collected a large library of such works at Sagres, from which he directed Portuguese exploration in the off-shore Atlantic and along the African coast. Columbus was an avid reader of the same accounts, which he used to support his theories about the wonders to be found in the Orient.

The eighteenth-century French Enlightenment was an effort to find rational explanations for natural phenomena that gave rise to most of the modern sciences, including geography. Typical of these early geographer/scientists was Charles Marie de la Condamine, who led a 1735–42 expedition to South America which produced the first maps of the Andean area based on accurate ground surveys. During the following century French expeditions produced maps and geographic descriptions from many different parts of the world, often as a by-product of French colonial expansion. However, the French efforts notwithstanding, it is the nineteenth-century German geographers Alexander von Humboldt and Carl Ritter who are credited with having first applied methods of scientific inquiry to the discipline and moved beyond description to ask: "Why?"

In the United States the development of geography as a separate discipline occurred toward the end of the nineteenth century at Harvard, Yale, Michigan, and Chicago, where scholars attempted to formulate theories to explain physical and social processes. However interesting these theories may have been for academic geographers, they had little or no impact on pre-university teaching, where the emphasis remained firmly grounded in memorization and description. Perhaps this is one reason why throughout much of the twentieth century, school geography in the United States has been relegated to a position of low or no priority. However, the 1980s and 1990s have seen a renaissance in the discipline, leading to the reappearance of geography in school curricula; the formation of more than fifty school-focused geographic alliances across the country; geography's inclusion as a core subject in the 1991 *Goals 2000: Educate America Act*; and the development of an Advanced Placement examination in human geography by the College Board, to name but a few milestone events.

Geography in the late twentieth century has moved far beyond the description implied by its name. Geography is commonly divided into two major branches: physical and human. *Physical geography* focuses on characteristics and processes of the natural world, such as landforms and the processes that create and change them; water, both fresh and saline, its supply and distribution; climate, with its long-term patterns and short-term events; the environment in all its dimensions, plants, animals, change, and risks. *Human geography* is concerned with the many aspects and manifestations of the human presence on Earth, past, present, and future. It includes such diverse subfields as population, urban, social, economic, behavioral, cultural, and political geography, to name but a few. The Association of American Geographers (AAG) currently recognizes forty-nine formal specialty groups within its membership. The division of geography into physical and human branches, each with many subfields, is not absolute, however. Each division is intricately intertwined with all others and human factors affect physical and vice versa. In fact, one of the major traditions of the discipline pivots around the interaction between human society and the natural environment. The many subfields of geography form a complex mosaic, but all are concerned with *space and place*. The unifying themes of geography are *location and landscape*, although a common fallacy is the oversimplification of these themes. Geographers are concerned with where things are located and what they are like, but "where" and "what" are only the beginning. Geographers also ask, Why is it there? What does its location mean? How does its location affect other places? How did the place get to be the way it is? Geographers are similarly concerned with how things are arranged, how they are organized, how they are connected—in other words, *patterns*. Patterns, in turn, bring the student of geography back to yet another level of questioning. Why are these patterns located where they are? What do they mean?

Understanding the scope of the field poses some challenges for the novice geographer. What body of knowledge defines the domain of geography? Geography is concerned with all phenomena that have a spatial dimension, that is, anything that can be identified in terms of location. In fact, geography is better defined in terms of its methodology and means of data presentation than by any particular body of knowledge. The methodology of geography is essentially questioning, Why is it located where it is? What does it mean? How did it get to be the way it is? The medium of data presentation most identified with geography is the map—an inherently spatial form of data display. All too often maps are seen by those outside the discipline as storehouses of factual information about places rather than tools that reveal insights about spatial relationships on Earth.

The lack of an easily identified content focus for the discipline, along with the public perception that geography is largely involved with collecting volumes of isolated facts about places, has caused professional geographers and geography educators to seek ways of better identifying the critical elements around which the discipline is organized and to find a way to make them more comprehensible to those outside the discipline.

Four Traditions

An early effort was by University of Chicago geographer William D. Pattison, who in 1964 attempted to bring "inner unity and outer intelligibility" to the discipline through an article entitled "The Four Traditions of Geography." Pattison's four traditions were spatial, area studies, man-land, and earth science (Pattison 1964).

The *spatial tradition* focuses on location and pattern and emphasizes the relationship of places in space. The spatial tradition has its origins in the writing of Claudius Ptolemy who collected data about locations around the Mediterranean such as sailing distances, the nature of landmarks, and the configuration of coasts. In the early days of the discipline maps that portrayed data collected by painstaking field work were used to identify patterns that could then be analyzed. Today, much of the mapping is carried out by computers, often using data that has been collected by satellites or other types of remote technology. The spatial tradition has application to urban planning, economic analysis, real estate appraisal, international affairs, military intelligence, and many other areas of modern life.

The *area studies tradition*, often referred to as "regional geography," is probably the subfield that is most closely associated with school geography. The largely descriptive works of Strabo fall into this tradition, as do most public school textbooks. The area studies tradition identifies broad general patterns of physical geography such as landforms, climate, soils, and vegetation along with distribution of culture traits such as language, religion, economy, architectural styles, economically useful plants and animals, and many other cultural elements associated with human occupation of Earth. Analysis of these patterns allows geographers to divide Earth into regions, or areas that share certain characteristics in common. Identification of global patterns also helps to identify and explain the distribution of physical and cultural phenomena. For example, identification of certain world-wide patterns of earthquake and volcanic activity (i.e., tectonic regions) helped geologists develop the theory of plate tectonics in the 1950s and 1960s. For political geographers maps of the distribution of Moslems, Jews, and Christians add greatly to our understanding of political instability in the Middle East or the Caucasus region. On a more local scale, regional and urban planners identify planning regions or city neighborhoods as units of analysis.

The *man-land tradition* arose out of early attempts to explain human behavior as a response to specific physical environments. This deterministic approach fell into disrepute among geographers in the early decades of the twentieth century but the search for understanding of how humans interact with their environment has continued with a new question,

"What is the role of human societies in modifying Earth's physical environments?" This tradition, of course, has great relevance for contemporary concerns about environmental issues such as air pollution and global warming, deforestation, biodiversity, and pollution of Earth's waters.

Finally, the *earth science tradition* embraces the interests of physical geographers at a variety of scales from global to extremely local. For example, some climatologists are interested in world-scale climate change processes while others are concerned with regional scale phenomena such as seasonal rainfall patterns. At the extremely local scale some climatologists study the distribution of microclimates around buildings or in similarly small areas. The earth science tradition shares broad areas of interest with other areas of physical science: geology, meteorology, pedology, and ecology, for example, but it differs from those in its emphasis on looking at the interrelationships of natural processes at or near the surface of Earth.

Five Themes

Pattison's traditions stimulated much discussion and argument and threads of his attempt at organization have persisted in current geographic thinking (Table 1.2). In particular geography educators have looked for coherent ways of introducing the variety of approaches utilized by practitioners of the discipline into the classroom.

The most successful response to this problem came in 1984 when a Joint Committee on Geographic Education of the National Council for Geographic Education (NCGE) and the Association of American Geographers (AAG), two leading professional organizations in the field, published the landmark *Guidelines for Geographic Education: Elementary and Secondary Schools*. The *Guidelines* emphasized that:

geography provides an effective method for asking questions about places on the earth and their relationships to the people who live in them. It involves a pattern of inquiry that *begins* with two essential questions: *Why* are such things located in these particular places and *how* do those particular places influence our lives? These two essential questions lead us to understandings and explanations of how and why the world in which we live can support us now and in the future. (Joint Committee 1984: 2)

The document went on to propose five fundamental themes in geography as a conceptual base for organizing geographic study. Reflecting threads of Pattison's traditions, the themes are *location*: position on Earth's surface; *place*: human and physical characteristics; *relationships within places*: humans and environments (frequently referred to as human-environment interaction); *movement*: humans interacting on Earth; and *regions*: how they form and change. Each theme provides a base for the investigation and questioning of the spatial phenomena and landscape patterns that define the world in which we live.

The "Five Themes" have emerged since 1984 as the principal organizational components in school geography. They appear in curriculum guides, are referred to in textbooks, and even appear in the opening pages of at least one world atlas. Their appeal comes from the relative ease with which they can be visualized. The Five Themes seem, at last, to have provided geographers with the easily-recognized public identification that has previously been lacking. If historians study the past, biologists study organisms, and geologists study rocks, geographers now claim location, place, human-environment relations, movement, and regions as their niche(s). The Four Traditions and the Five Themes contributed greatly to clarifying the image of geography. The next step was to identify the knowledge base and skills that a geographically informed person should have. This process was facilitated by the inclusion of geography among the core subjects of the *Goals 2000: Educate America Act* (Public Law 103–227).

National Geography Standards

The culmination of the current renaissance in geography education came in 1994 with the publication of *Geography for Life: National Geography Standards*. The standards propose voluntary benchmarks for what geography students in the United States should know and be able to do. As such, the standards (Table 1.1) provide a context for geographic study and research at all grade levels. "The outcome of *Geography for Life* is a geographically informed person (1) who sees meaning in the arrangement of things in space; (2) who sees relations between people, places, and environments; (3) who uses geographic skills; and (4) who applies spatial and ecological perspectives to life situations" (*Geography for Life* 1994: p. 34).

Geography, with its methodology of inquiry and its broad spatial scope, offers powerful learning opportunities that have real world applications. However, failure to exercise critical thinking skills has often relegated geography to a position of low priority in the curriculum. Absent from critical thinking, geography risks becoming little more than rote memorization of facts with no analytical context. Such an approach not only numbs the mind but also robs students of the opportunity to think about the world in which they live and to prepare themselves for active, participatory citizenship.

Barbara J. Winston, professor emeritus of Geography and Environmental Studies at Northeastern Illinois University in Chicago, argues that

Table 1.1
Geography for Life: **The Eighteen Standards**

The geographically informed person knows and understands:

The World in Spatial Terms
1. How to use maps and other geographic representations, tools, and technologies to acquire, process, and report information from a spatial perspective
2. How to use mental maps to organize information about people, places, and environments in a spatial context
3. How to analyze the spatial organization of people, places, and environments on Earth's surface

Places and Regions
4. The physical and human characteristics of places
5. That people create regions to interpret Earth's complexity
6. How culture and experience influence people's perceptions of places and regions

Physical Systems
7. The physical processes that shape the patterns of Earth's surface
8. The characteristics and spatial distribution of ecosystems on Earth's surface

Human Systems
9. The characteristics, distribution, and migration of human populations on Earth's surface
10. The characteristics, distribution, and complexity of Earth's cultural mosaics
11. The patterns and networks of economic interdependence on Earth's surface
12. The processes, patterns, and functions of human settlement
13. How the forces of cooperation and conflict among people influence the division and control of Earth's surface

Environment and Society
14. How human actions modify the physical environment
15. How physical systems affect human systems
16. The changes that occur in the meaning, use, distribution, and importance of resources

The Uses of Geography
17. How to apply geography to interpret the past
18. How to apply geography to interpret the present and plan for the future

Source: *Geography for Life: National Geography Standards 1994*, 34–35.

geographic knowledge and skills help citizens be better informed on a wide range of issues such as: (1) understanding the impact of overseas events and policies on the United States and the world; (2) evaluating the United States response to global issues; (3) assessing the voting records of elected representatives; (4) promoting more enlightened views on cultural diversity and reducing stereotyping; and (5) contributing to solving problems related to community and regional planning, and dealing with complex local and regional issues such as preservation of open space or transportation development. Winston also notes that the geographer's ability to read and understand maps may help them make critical analyses of information presented in the news media (Winston 1986: 43). In sum, students who gain a knowledge of geography and of the techniques used by geographers to present and analyze data will be well prepared to take an active role as citizens, both directly as participants in civic activities and indirectly as informed critics of government policy.

WHAT IS CRITICAL THINKING IN GEOGRAPHY?

Today's students live in a world filled with polarizing issues—ethnic and religious tensions, environmental degradation, population growth, climate change, social and economic inequity—the list is almost endless. These topics are controversial and the public is presented with widely divergent views regarding their urgency and what measures, if any, should be taken to ameliorate them. All of these issues fall within the domain of geographic inquiry because each has a spatial dimension, that is, each occurs in a place or places that can be identified. But it is not enough merely to ask, Where is it? Students must be encouraged to ask, as well, Why is it occurring where it is? What are the consequences for that place, for other places, for me? Good geography involves cultivation and practice of habits of critical thinking.

The quartet of geographic skills dubbed by Christopher Salter (1989: 20–22) as OSAE—observation, speculation, analysis, and evaluation—speaks to the heart of critical thinking. Observation involves the identification of the issue in terms of physical and cultural elements that make up the spatial context in which the issue exists. Speculation is best characterized as raising geographic questions, such as, Why do real estate prices vary with location? Analysis leads students to consider what evidence is required in order to address the questions raised, to determine sources of data, and to deal with conflicting information. The final step, evaluation, calls upon students to measure all the evidence accumulated, make informed decisions about what to do or believe, and identify new questions that call for further inquiry.

While critical thinking involves questioning, not all questions require the reflection and evaluation that characterize critical thinking. In an attempt to categorize types of questions, Frances Slater (1993: 9) sees a continuum from recall to critical thinking (Table 1.2). Slater emphasizes learning through inquiry and stresses the importance of carefully crafted questions that demand more than simple recall. Higher order questioning involves students in observation, classification, analysis, reasoning, and evaluation.

Table 1.2
Encouraging Critical Thinking Through Questions

Closed			Open	Critical Thinking
Demanding recall	Encouraging classification and ordering	Encouraging the use of data to draw conclusions	Encouraging awareness of the limitations of the evidence or evaluation of evidence	Encouraging an awareness of the processes of reasoning to be used

Source: Slater (1993), 9.

In order to frame good questions students must have a foundation in the basic concepts of geography. It has already been established that a common central theme of geography is location, but students need a vocabulary of the concepts of spatial analysis in order to recognize and pose good geographic questions. A spatial vocabulary begins from a base that includes such terms as location, place, size, scale, distance, direction, distribution, density, pattern, accessibility, diffusion, and interaction. Each of these concepts represents the nucleus of questions that can shed light on the issue at hand. Meaningful questions cannot be posed without an understanding of these and other basic concepts:

- location—position on Earth's surface relative to a grid (e.g., latitude and longitude) or to other places. Where is it? Why is it here? Is it found elsewhere?
- place—a location distinguished in terms of physical and human characteristics that make it unique. What is it like there? What factors have influenced it?
- size—areal extent or numerical magnitude of spatial phenomena. How large (or small) is it? How many are there? Has it always been so?
- scale—degree of generalization; distance on a map relative to actual Earth distance; size of unit under consideration, for example, global versus local. Is the scale of the map or data appropriate for the purpose of inquiry? How would a different scale influence understanding?
- distance—separation between two points in terms of a linear unit such as miles or a relative unit such as time. How far is it? How does distance affect connections to other points? How does distance affect communication?
- direction—position on Earth in terms of the cardinal points (north, south, east, west). Where is it?
- distribution—arrangement of phenomena in a given area. Is the arrangement concentrated or dispersed? What factors have influenced this arrangement?
- density—number of a phenomenon within a given areal unit (e.g., $\#/mi^2$); an average. Is the density high or low? Does the implied generalization disguise important variation?

- pattern—arrangement of phenomena in terms of design (e.g., linear, clustered, random). Is there a pattern in the distribution? What factors have influenced the formation of this pattern? Has this pattern always been present? How/why has it changed?

- accessibility—relative ease with which a given place can be reached. Is it easily reached or is it isolated? Has it always been so? What factors have influenced its accessibility? What is the effect of its accessibility/isolation?

- diffusion—the spread or movement of phenomena (e.g., products, ideas, technology) between places. Is this place a source or target of diffusion? Why/why not? Has it always been so? What factors of change are at work?

- interaction—the degree to which places are connected. How is this place connected to other places? How/in what ways is this place influenced by other places? How/why have connections changed over time?

These concepts and others lay a foundation for seeing meaning in where and how things occur in a spatial context. Such understanding, representing the heart of geographic knowledge, is reached only through reasoned inquiry. Reasoned inquiry lies at the heart of critical thinking.

WHY ARE CRITICAL THINKING SKILLS USEFUL IN GEOGRAPHY?

Both the 1984 *Guidelines* and the 1994 *Geography for Life* speak to the importance of cultivating geographic skills. These skills enable us to identify, organize, and apply geographic information, which in turn leads to informed geographic decision-making. People make geographic decisions every day of their lives, although often without recognizing the nature of the thinking process involved. For example: What is the best route from home to school? Where shall we go on vacation? Where is the best place to shop for new athletic shoes? Geographic decision-making plays an active role in government and business choices as well: Where will the new interstate highway be built? How can we protect our community's fresh water supply? Does our community need a new elementary school? Why have so many stores on Main Street gone out of business?

The basic skills identified in *Geography for Life* (adapted from those presented in the *Guidelines*) are

- asking geographic questions
- acquiring geographic information
- organizing geographic information
- analyzing geographic information
- answering geographic questions

Asking geographic questions, grounded in sound geographic concepts, has been discussed above. However, moving forward toward answering these questions involves *acquiring geographic information,* which requires the selection, manipulation, and interpretation of data obtained from diverse sources. Quantitative (numerical) data include such sources as maps, graphs, photographs, population and other censuses, economic and trade statistics, information on installed infrastructure (e.g., electric generating capacity, paved roads, hospitals and other health facilities, and educational facilities), health statistics (e.g., life expectancy, infant mortality, and incidence of certain diseases), environmental statistics (e.g., air quality indicators, fresh water availability, natural hazard occurrences), and a wide variety of other quantitative information that can be used to determine the spatial distribution of relative social and economic well-being.

Geographers also rely on primary data collected directly through field observations. While their travel opportunities may be more limited, students, too, can gather field data in order to answer geographic questions. For example, students can conduct surveys on consumer shopping habits or product preferences. They can record traffic volume on streets near their school in order to examine variations in patterns and frequency. They can prepare and administer questionnaires within the school in order to compare characteristics of the school community with those of a larger population (e.g., city, state, country).

Geographers draw upon qualitative (descriptive) data as well. Qualitative sources may include first-person accounts of travel or life in a foreign country or at a different time in history, local histories, diaries and journals, business/commercial directories, tourist and other guide books, and similar materials. Qualitative data may also be gathered directly through personal interviews with relatives, elderly members of the community, new arrivals in the community, or students in another part of the state or country via Internet electronic mail. It may also be collected through personal observation.

Acquiring geographic information calls for use of critical thinking skills. Selection of data, regardless of the source, involves careful evaluation. Students must consider such issues as reliability, comparability, bias, and appropriateness for the purpose at hand. Reliability involves assessing the source of the data against known standards. Does the data reflect a broad survey or merely a limited sample? For example, the U.S. Census Bureau (http://www.census.gov) is generally regarded to be a reliable source, but a survey published by a local civic organization might require close scrutiny. In order to compare data from different sources or for different time periods, it is important that all data reflect a common standard in terms of units or methods of collection. For example, climate data (http://www.worldclimate.com) gathered from two graphs, one showing inches and Fahrenheit, the other millimeters and Celsius, cannot be immediately compared because different and incompatible systems of measurement have been used. It is especially important that the source of data be known as well as the purpose for which the data was collected. While one might anticipate bias in qualitative data, quantitative data can also, by selective omission, project bias. For example, data reflecting community opinion about the location of a landfill may lack objectivity if the survey from which the data was drawn included responses from only selected interest groups. Finally, data must be appropriate for the inquiry being conducted. For example, a statistical summary of ethnic groups in the former Yugoslavia might be much less effective than a map showing the distributions of these groups in explaining the pattern of conflict that led to the break-up of the country. (http://www.lib.utexas.edu/Libs/PCL/Map_collection/Map_collection. html). Just as students apply critical thinking skills to the evaluation of an issue or problem, so too must they evaluate, question, and reflect on the data that is chosen to support an inquiry into the issue. Data is not inherently objective. Students must learn to apply a critical filter to all information.

Once data relevant to the issue or problem under investigation has been gathered, this information must be sorted, classified, organized, and presented in ways that support evaluation from multiple perspectives so that objective decisions can be made. *Organizing geographic information* can take many forms. Organization of data should be systematic, with a focus on clarity and objectivity. Students need to be sensitive to the fact that sorting and classifying data in a particular way can introduce bias, thus impeding critical analysis. Once sorted, an appropriate presentation format must be selected. Maps are most often associated with geographic information but geographers rely upon other presentation types as well, including graphs, tables, diagrams, drawings, and photographs. Narrative description and explanation also play an important part in the presentation of geographic information. Within each presentation type, further selection is required. For example, it is important to select a map of a scale appropriate to the data to be mapped. Endangered wetlands in the United States might be shown on a small scale national map, but human intrusion into the Everglades ecosystem would be better represented on a large scale map of southern Florida (see maps for 1900, 1953, and 1973 at http://141.232.1.11/org/bcb/3_bcblinks.html). Likewise, the type of graph selected must be consistent with the data being presented—bar graphs for comparison, line graphs for change or trend over time, and pie graphs to show percentages of a whole. Selection of appropriate presentation tools calls for critical thinking skills to ensure clarity and objectivity.

Asking geographic questions and acquiring and organizing geographic information set the stage for analysis. *Analyzing geographic information* calls for the full range of critical thinking skills—thinking, reasoning, questioning, and evaluating the information presented. Returning to geography's central concepts, students should look for patterns, associations, connections, interaction, and evidence of change. Geographic analysis does not always produce immediate results. Students must be prepared to face more questions as analysis progresses. This is clear evidence of the close link between geographic inquiry and critical thinking. For example, after observing the changing pattern over time in population growth rates in the political units making up the Washington, D.C. metropolitan area (http://www.census.gov), a new question begins to form: What changes in population structure might account for decline in some areas and increase in others? Further, what factors might account for changes in the population structure? Is this pattern unique to Washington, D.C. or is it repeated in other metropolitan areas?

The final step in the process of geographic inquiry is answering geographic questions. *Answering geographic questions* enables students to make informed decisions, arrive at conclusions, or form generalizations—all goals of critical thinking. Having exercised skills of critical thinking in order to answer the initial and subsequent questions raised, students gain confidence in their ability to solve problems and share knowledge. They appreciate that most issues do not have simple, direct answers but rather have complex, multifaceted layers reflecting different interests and points of view. Once students begin to view questions as opportunities rather than assignments, they have begun to take charge of their own learning.

HOW DO CRITICAL THINKING SKILLS CONTRIBUTE TO CULTIVATING A GEOGRAPHIC PERSPECTIVE?

Good geography employs critical thinking. Critical thinking requires an open and questioning mind. The critical thinker, whatever the subject at hand, is constantly seeking explanations for what she or he observes: Why is this so? What information was used to derive that conclusion? Are there other interpretations that might be made from the same data? Was the information gathered and presented from an unbiased perspective? These are the kinds of questions that a geographer asks, but it is the focus of the questions that makes them geographic, not their nature. Thus, a critical thinker is well-prepared to become a good geographer. The only ingredient that is required is to cultivate an appreciation for the kinds of questions geographers ask.

A geographer constantly asks questions about what he or she reads, sees, or is told. These questions will be oriented toward the traditions and themes that were discussed earlier in this chapter: location, spatial relations, movement, human-environment relationships, the nature of places, and regions. To find the answers to these questions requires highly developed skills of observation, familiarity with techniques of data collection, analysis, and presentation and a healthy sense of skepticism. All of these traits are developed in the process of learning to become a critical thinker. However, not all critical thinkers will be geographers—they must be trained to look in the right places and to ask the right kinds of questions. The following chapters in this book will deal with these issues.

REFERENCES

Geography for Life: National Geography Standards 1994. (1994) Geography Education Standards Project. Washington, DC: National Geographic Society.

Hill, A. David. (1994) "Geography Instructional Materials for Standards-Based Education" in *A Decade of Reform in Geographic Education: Inventory and Prospect* edited by Robert S. Bednarz and James F. Petersen. Indiana, PA: National Council for Geographic Education.

Joint Committee on Geographic Education. (1984) *Guidelines for Geographic Education: Elementary and Secondary Schools.* Washington, DC and Macomb, IL: Association of American Geographers and National Council for Geographic Education.

Pattison, William D. (1964) "The Four Traditions of Geography," *The Journal of Geography,* 63: 211–216.

Salter, Christopher L. (1989) "Teaching Geography Across the Curriculum," *NASSP Bulletin: The Journal for Middle and High School Administrators,* 73: 521, 19–24.

Sayers, Dorothy L. (1979) "The Lost Tools of Learning," *National Review* (January 19, 1979): 90–99.

Slater, Frances. (1993) *Learning Through Geography.* Indiana, PA: National Council for Geographic Education.

Winston, Barbara J. (1986) "Teaching and Learning in Geography," in *Social Studies and Social Sciences: A Fifty-Year Perspective* edited by Stanley P. Wronski and Donald H. Bragaw. Washington, DC: National Council for the Social Studies.

Primary Sources for Geographers

2

Geography is related to many other fields of study. These fields include sciences such as geology, meteorology, soil science, biology and hydrology, which most often are part of the study of physical geography. Human geographers use data and concepts from social sciences such as economics, anthropology, linguistics, political science, psychology, and sociology as well as material from humanities disciplines such as history, languages, and literature. Because of its diversity geography depends on an extremely wide array of data sources to describe different parts of the world, to identify relationships among different parts of Earth, and to explain the processes that account for where things are and why they occur as they do. Data sources are often placed in the following categories: primary, original, or secondary.

PRIMARY SOURCES, ORIGINAL SOURCES, AND SECONDARY SOURCES

Primary data sources used by geographers (Table 2.1) may be written in narrative form as notes, diaries, or other accounts of important events or processes, they may be handdrawn field maps or published base maps, or they may be quantitative information such as census counts or temperature and precipitation data. Audio or video recordings, photographs, and digitized data from remote sensing can also be primary data. The thing that makes the data useful for geographers is that it tells us something about Earth and its human population. Primary sources need not be original, but they should have been carefully compiled or pre-

Table 2.1
Primary Data Sources Used by Geographers

- letters, diaries, journals, field notes, and other written accounts that describe landscapes, native peoples, economic activities, or other information that is of potential interest for geographers

- data collected in the field by the investigator, such as field maps, interviews, surveys, photographs, or digital images

- data on human conditions such as censuses, economic production data, literacy rates and levels of education, health conditions and/or care, and type and quality of housing, which provide information on demographic, social, economic, or other human characteristics of a region, country, or group of people

- data on physical conditions such as temperature, precipitation, wind, cloud cover, soil characteristics and type, elevation, slope, drainage, vegetation cover, and other information relating to the physical conditions of the area being studied

- maps of certain types such as field maps, topographic maps (for place names, landforms, stream patterns, transport systems, etc.), and photo maps

- photographs, digital images, motion pictures, videos, and audio tapes (if they contain relevant information)

- aerial photographs, satellite images, and other remotely sensed data in photographic or digital form

pared from original information so they have a high probability of being accurate and free of bias. Original sources are materials that come directly from the individual (or instrument) that collected them. These include ships' logs, scientific field notes, first-person accounts of travel or investigation, original photographs (ground or aerial), satellite images and digital data, and original data that is collected on the ground by researchers and/or instruments such as the census-takers' reports from a national census or climate data gathered at a weather station, for example. Original sources are often kept in archives, special collection libraries, or other secure places. Access to originals is often restricted, but microfilm copies, photocopies, or printed versions may be available. Original sources are primary sources but not all primary sources are original sources as we shall see below.

Secondary sources, which are not a focus of this book, include second-hand reports such as might be contained in biographies, condensed or abstracted travel accounts, general histories or geographies, data that have been condensed or statistically manipulated, or any other source that has been modified in some substantive manner or that condenses or summarizes from primary or original sources. The assumption is that such data, while useful, may contain errors or interpretations that have been added in the course of their publication or presentation. Written documents may have been abridged, taken out of context, or have had errors introduced in the process of reproduction or quotation. None of these limitations mean that information from secondary sources is not valid or potentially valuable, but it does warn the user to be aware of possible errors, omissions, or biases that might be introduced beyond those that were inherent in the primary source from which they were derived.

The following example illustrates the difference between primary, original, and secondary geographic sources. Christopher Columbus kept a diary of his first voyage of discovery to the New World in 1492 (diary excerpts are on the Internet at the Medieval Sourcebook site: http://www.fordham.edu/halsall/source/columbus1.html). Columbus presented the original of this invaluable document to the King and Queen of Spain when he returned from his epic journey and a hand-written copy was made for him. The diary is unquestionably an original source and a primary source. If the copy were perfectly made, it could be considered a primary source as well, but it would be necessary to compare the two documents to determine if they contain identical information because the person who made the copy might have made errors in transcription.

Unfortunately, both the original Columbus diary and the copy have been lost for centuries. We now depend on an abstract, or summary, of the diary made by the Dominican friar Bartolome de las Casas probably about forty years after Columbus made his voyage. No one knows for sure how much of the original diary Las Casas may have left out, what he summarized or took out of context, and what he copied verbatim. Also left open is the possibility of transcription errors that may have been made as Las Casas copied from the Columbus diary. The Las Casas version of Columbus's diary is clearly not an original source. If the original were still in existence, the Las Casas copy would be a secondary source and probably of little interest for historians, geographers, and other researchers. However, since the Las Casas transcription is the only contemporary copy of the Columbus diary that remains in existence, it may be considered a primary source document for the Columbus voyage, even though it is clearly far less than the original (Dunn and Kelley 1989).

USES AND RELIABILITY OF
PRIMARY SOURCES IN GEOGRAPHY

Geographers use primary sources to learn about Earth. Primary data about the physical world such as rainfall and temperature records, distribution of earthquakes and volcanic activity, records of vegetation types, flood records, or soil characteristics all contribute to understanding the natural processes that shape the different parts of Earth. Data on population distribution, type of economy, quality of life, health status, education, and a wide range of other social and economic indicators are essential for understanding the different ways in which humans use natural resources. They also give clues to how well or poorly they live. Historical records of all sorts, from surveyor's reports of vegetation and other patterns of landscape to aerial photographs taken decades ago, help geographers and other scientists discover how Earth is changing and why (see the USGS Earthshots: Satellite Images of Environmental Change site at http://edcwww.cr.usgs.gov/earthshots/slow/tableofcontents for satellite images that illustrate environmental change over the past twenty years).

Generally, information from primary sources is preferred for all of the purposes noted above. That is because primary sources are less likely to contain errors than data that has been processed in some way and because the primary sources contain basic data that can be interpreted or, in the case of numerical data, manipulated statistically to reveal useful and interesting trends or details. Photographs and maps that are simplified or generalized contain less information than the primary sources from which they were derived. In the case of historical materials, the primary sources may provide the earliest recorded impressions of what a place looks like, or they may provide benchmark data that can be used to determine what kind of change has taken place or is taking place in a particular area. Secondary sources may provide the same information but they are considered to be less reliable because the information has been modified by a second party, as in the case of the Las Casas abstract of the Columbus diary.

As noted above, primary sources are usually considered to be better than secondary sources for most purposes. Nevertheless, they do present some problems for the user. Perhaps the most obvious problem is the reliability of first-person accounts. Returning to the example of Columbus, when he arrived in the Caribbean in 1492 he literally did not know where he was. He was convinced that he had sailed to Asia and many of his interpretations were shaped by that error. First person accounts may be interesting, but they are not necessarily reliable. Students who use such accounts must read with caution and look for inconsistencies in narration and reports of unlikely events that are clues to possible errors of fact or interpretation.

With respect to statistical sources, most of us are familiar with the computer user's warning: "Garbage in, garbage out." No matter how sophisticated the analysis or how powerful the computer, the results of analysis of numerical data are only as good as the information from which the analysis was produced. Data that contains bias, is incomplete, was recorded incorrectly, or is based on misleading or confusingly worded questions is reduced in value or useless as a tool for interpreting processes of change on Earth. For these reasons, it is important to know the conditions under which the data was collected, including the definitions of certain terms used in censuses, instructions to the data collectors and, if a sample survey was used, how the samples were constructed.

Even data collected by scientific instruments may present problems. Rainfall records may be increased or reduced depending on where the rainfall gauge is located. A thermometer located near an asphalt street or parking lot will register higher and lower extremes than one in a grassy area, and a sunny location will get much hotter than one in the shade. Los Angeles presents an example of how location can affect weather and climate data. The airport, where official climate data is recorded, is located in west Los Angeles, close to the coast. Cool ocean breezes keep average summer temperatures at the airport about 10°F cooler than locations even a few blocks farther east and more distant from the coast. Most people in Los Angeles live inland away from the coast. For them temperatures recorded at the airport have little or no relevance, and the same might be said for someone who was planning a visit to the city and who wanted to know what kind of weather to prepare for (this bit of information may be tested by going to a primary source, the National Atmospheric and Oceanic Administration at http://www.nwsla.noaa.gov, and checking temperature data for different locations in the greater Los Angeles urban area).

One would expect that photographs and maps, which seem to represent the world "as it is," would be free from bias and error. However, no map can include everything that appears in the area of coverage. The cartographer must decide what elements are most important for the purpose of the map and which items may be left out. *Thematic maps* show specific distributions, for example climate, land use, or some other phenomenon that may be of interest. They usually omit any information that is not directly related to the theme of the map or necessary to show distributions (such as continents, oceans, national boundaries, and the geographic grid). For these reasons, thematic maps are generally considered to be secondary sources.

Base maps such as the *topographic maps* produced by government agencies in the United States and other countries (see Chapter 3 for a short list of these agencies) include a wide range of cultural data such as roads, railroads, buildings, airports, and key landmarks such as water towers, reservoirs and dams, beacons and lighthouses, bridges, schools, churches, and cemeteries. Physical information includes lakes, rivers and streams, landforms and elevations (shown by contour lines), vegetation cover, and many other features. However, a great deal of information is omitted or generalized in order to keep the map from becoming too crowded or busy. It is easy to see what has been included in a map, but the only way to know what has been left off is actually to visit the map site or to look at aerial photographs or satellite images of the area and compare them with the map. The choice of what information to include and omit from a map affects its usefulness and the user should be aware in a general way of what is included and what has been left off a map to obtain the greatest value from it.

In a technical sense topographic maps are secondary sources because there is a selection process for data to be included on the map. However, many geographers consider such maps to be primary sources because they provide faithful portrayals of landforms and other physical characteristics along with an assortment of cultural features that makes up the base data of the map. Old editions of topographic maps (some early European topographic maps are now over two centuries old) are invaluable historic records of past landscapes. However, as noted above, the user must be aware that some details of the landscape were omitted from the map.

Even aerial photographs and satellite images present problems. Conditions may change rapidly and the image, unless it is being used for historical comparison, should be recent. Whatever the image, if it does not carry an indication of the location it covers and a date, it is virtually worthless. Location is fundamental for geographers and the photograph should carry an identifying place name as well as approximate geographical coordinates (latitude and longitude) so the subject can easily be found on a map. The year of the photograph is a benchmark that allows the user to place the photograph in its historic context and one should know the time of year when an image was generated because certain patterns occur seasonally. Certain features are easier to see in mid-latitude winter, for example, when deciduous trees are bare of leaves (the same principle applies in seasonal tropical areas, where trees often lose their leaves in the dry season). Some objects may be difficult to identify on a normal photograph, such as a house tucked away in the forest. On the other hand, infra-red films and sensors can register the heat generated by a warm building in winter even if it is not easily seen on film that is sensitive to visible light. Scale can also be a problem with photographs, which undergo slight distortion between the center and the edges because of the curvature of the lens and the changing perspective from the point where the photograph is centered. There are ways of compensating for or correcting these problems but one must know they exist before they may be dealt with.

Finally, there is the issue of *geographic scale* and the level of aggregation of data. In a strict sense, the primary data from a census or survey is the raw information contained in the census questionnaires or survey documents. However, these sources may be confidential. For example, the raw data from the Untied States census (the actual census takers' records) are not available to the public until eighty years after the census was made. Even if the information were available to the public, for most purposes the time required for assembling it into a usable form would be prohibitive. Thus, researchers generally rely on statistical compilations of the original data. The choice of how this information is aggregated will determine the scale at which the researcher can work. If census data are available only at the state level, for example, it will be impossible to see patterns of population distribution within a state. Data by census tract may be very useful if one wants to see where different socio-economic groups live within a city or metropolitan area but they would be difficult to handle if one were interested in state-level distributions. County data might be more useful for that scale of analysis.

PRIMARY SOURCES AND SCIENTIFIC
DATA COLLECTION FOR GEOGRAPHY

Data sources have changed over time as technology has progressed. Two hundred years ago, Lewis and Clark made sketch maps and drawings and kept hand-written diaries and notebooks to record the scientific discoveries of their famous expedition to the Pacific Coast. They collected and dried plant specimens and caught wildlife, some of which was returned live to Washington, D.C. However, many of the biological specimens were kept as skeletons and dried skins that were carried along with the expedition until it returned to the United States. Latitude was calculated using a *sextant* and longitude was determined with a *chronometer*. Lewis and Clark made careful observations of wildlife, vegetation, and landforms, and plotted the courses of rivers they followed. These observations were made in accord with the instructions the explorers received from President Thomas Jefferson, which were to collect as much information about the land and native people as they could and to record information from which an accurate map of their route could be made (see the Rojomo site at http://www.mt.net/~rojomo/landc.htm?12,44 for the instructions that were given to Lewis and Clark by President Jefferson).

Today an expedition to Antarctica, for example, would carry an array of sophisticated instruments to measure every conceivable natural characteristic of the area and use modern *global positioning systems* (GPS) to determine exact geographic locations and surface elevations. Any biological specimens that were collected would be sent back live, if possible, for classification and analysis. If this were not possible, specimens would be frozen for later shipment to laboratories for examination using high powered microscopes and chemical analyses.

In the areas of social analysis Lewis and Clark lived with some native Americans and visited others. They reported what they observed of native habits, commenting on agricultural practices, hunting techniques, food preparation, belief systems, and dozens of other aspects of their life, and they sent examples of their weapons, tools, and other artifacts to Washington along with the biological specimens noted above.

In modern times social and economic data is still sometimes collected in the field by researchers, but it is more common to use surveys, censuses, or official reports from government agencies to learn about how people live. Many times the data collection procedures are standardized by international organizations such as the United Nations in the hope that information will be comparable for all countries that participate. However, there is no mechanism to enforce such standardized procedures and international comparisons may be affected by differences in the standards used to collect and/or analyze it or by the currency of the information made available. The World Bank web site (http://www.worldbank.org/) contains a discussion of some of these data problems on its page titled "Primary Data Documentation," which can be downloaded as a PDF file.

Remote sensing, the collection of data from cameras and other sensors in airplanes satellites, and other remotely located platforms, also is used to obtain data on social and economic characteristics of human population on Earth. Remote sensing is especially useful for observing the spatial distributions of human activities on Earth, which is a special interest of geographers. The "What's New In Remote Sensing" page (http://www.vtt.fi/aut/rs/virtual/new.html) provides links to many interesting sites dealing with remote sensing. One of the links at this site, the European Space Agency, offers a series of classroom exercises for students to learn about remote sensing and its applications (http://seaspace.esa.int:8000/exercises).

Analytical techniques also have become much more sophisticated as knowledge about the world improves, as the amount of data available increases, and as computers make it possible to process that data easily and rapidly. *Geographic information systems* (GIS) allow geographers to overlay vast amounts of data obtained by remote sensing and to compare it, providing new insights into how we humans use and modify Earth. There are many private companies that offer GIS packages and most university geography programs have GIS courses. To access information on these resources try the GeographyAbout.com page (http://geography.about.com/) on GIS. This site provides links to other sites and also provides a brief introduction to GIS technology.

Early geographers offered speculative explanations of change on Earth that were based on legend, superstition, or intuition. Modern geographers publish rigorous scientific studies that are derived from analysis of large amounts of data. The data come from a multitude of sources, including those mentioned above, and the theories developed from that data are subject to continual testing and reevaluation in the light of new information. New data may lead to development of alternative *hypotheses* that are perceived to offer more satisfactory explanations of natural and/or social processes on Earth. This continuous testing and reevaluation of explanations for geographic phenomena are part of the *scientific method*. The scientific method, in turn, is closely linked with the strategies of critical thinking: comparing and contrasting, sequencing, classifying, identifying cause and effect, problem-solving, and decision-making. (There are many web sites dealing with scientific method and hypothesis building. The following site is part of "Fundamentals of Physical Geography," an Internet-based course developed by Dr. Michael Pidwirny of Okanagan University College in British Columbia, Canada. This page discusses scientific method in the context of physical geography: http://www.geog.ouc.bc.ca/physgeog/contents/3a.html.)

The scientific method depends on accurate data for its effectiveness. If data are absent or incorrect, the conclusions drawn from research will be questionable at best and at worst wrong. Therefore, any effective geographic investigation begins with a strategy for obtaining the most accurate data available on the subject at hand. Primary sources generally offer the best possibility for obtaining data of the quality, reliability, and replicability needed to support the rigorous testing required by the scientific method.

FIRST-PERSON ACCOUNTS

Many travelers keep diaries, notes, or other informal records of the things they observe as they visit new and strange places. Geographers and other scientists generally keep fairly extensive field notes from which they later draw conclusions or extract information. Some of the records kept by Meriwether Lewis and William Clark, cited in the previous section, are field notes but the documents that are usually reproduced are the journals kept by the expedition leaders and their men (see "Along the Trail with Lewis and Clark," a site created by students at Washington State University, for excerpts from the Lewis and Clark Expedition journals at http://lewisandclark.com). This is because field notes are not usually kept in narrative form so they are much less interesting to read than journals which record the day to day events of travel and exploration. Some other journals and informal travel diaries available on the Internet are noted in the sections that follow.

Both informal travel diaries and explorers' or scientists' journals may provide useful geographic insights, but they are quite different. Geographers and explorers generally provide more thorough accounts, and often take pains to note details about the landscape, including plants and animals, landforms, climate, native people, and other features because they know they will have to prepare a formal report on what they have observed in their travels. Diaries and personal notes are kept for the satisfaction of the individuals who make them and they are generally less systematic in their recording of geographic information than journals.

Explorers and Geographers

Often geography is equated with exploration and some of the most compelling accounts in the history of geography, namely the diary of Columbus's first voyage, come from explorers. Unquestionably, exploration expands our knowledge of Earth. However, most explorers are motivated by non-scientific objectives. Explorers want to forge new trails, to go where no one has gone before. Columbus was the first European to see the Caribbean. Magellan commanded the first fleet to sail around the world. Vasco da Gama was the first European to sail around Africa to India. Roald Amundsen was the first person to stand at the South Pole and Admiral Richard Byrd was the first to fly over it. In their quest to be first, explorers may also be searching for knowledge that will have military or economic value and their observations are clearly useful for geographers and other scientists. Nevertheless, explorers generally are not trained to collect data of explanatory value nor are they trained to seek explanations for what they see. Columbus, for example, believed he had found cinnamon trees in the Caribbean, but none grew there at the time of his voyage. If Columbus had known more about botany or if there had been a botanist in his crew, he probably would not have made this mistake. It is the quest that motivates explorers. Scientific objectives are secondary and often included only because they justify the exploration to fund-granting organizations and individuals.

Geographers, on the other hand, along with natural historians, geologists, anthropologists, and other students of the natural world and its people, are trained to collect data carefully, recording all of the conditions under which it is gathered, and to use these data to improve our understanding of natural and social processes. Their methods and objectives differ in important ways from those of explorers. They take copious notes, collect samples of plants, animals, rocks, soil, and whatever human artifacts may be available, and carefully document the exact location and circumstances under which they collected specimens or made observations. Geographers think comparatively, trying to relate what they observe to other situations they may have seen or read about. How are two places similar and why? How are they different and what might explain the differences? What are the important processes that shape the landscapes I am seeing? These are the questions geographers ask as they collect data. As fascinating and compelling as first-person accounts of exploration may be, the often prosaic reports from the field of scientists frequently may be more useful primary sources for understanding the world.

NPR's "Radio Expeditions" series (http://www.npr.org/programs/RE/), which aired in 1999, is an online audio presentation that deals with exploration and research. Each program, which lasts for about ten minutes, features an important event of exploration or scientific discovery. These programs are not primary sources in the strict sense, because they are, for the most part, second-hand reports. However, a few of the programs feature interviews with living scientists and explorers or quotations from their writings. After a class discussion of the difference between scientific research and exploration, students could evaluate which type of activity a program describes and explain why they chose the classification they did. As an alternative, students could report on what the scientist or explorer had to say about her or his work.

Diaries and Travel Narratives

Diaries and travel narratives are personal accounts generally written by non-specialists who may be keen observers of the world. The travel account of Marco Polo is one of the earliest such documents (see the Silk Road Foundation page on Marco Polo at http://www.silk-road.com/artl/marcopolo.shtml or the Geography Site Marco Polo biographical sketch at http://geography.about.com/library/weekly/aa081798.htm). It is still read by historians and geographers who seek knowledge of Asia as it was nearly 800 years ago; and the veracity of Polo's account is still hotly debated (see USA Today Book Shelf for a review of a book that argues Marco Polo never went to China at http://www.usatoday.com/life/enter/books/leb282.htm). More contemporary examples of personal accounts are diaries of pioneers as they traveled across the United States on the Oregon Trail or to California during the Gold Rush, reports from people who have visited foreign lands, or accounts of some natural disaster. All fall into the category of personal accounts. Many such accounts may be found on the Internet. The Library of Western Fur Trade Historical Source Documents (http://www.xmission.com/~drudy/mtman/mmarch.html) contains links to many excellent examples of this genre.

For students who live in communities located near pioneer trails or in other places for which personal accounts may be available (large cities, for example) it may be possible to use historical accounts to identify elements of landscape change between the time of the report and the present. Questions that might be asked about rural areas are: How has vegetation changed? Are any of the old landscapes preserved? If farms are mentioned, are crops still the same? Are pioneer travel routes paralleled by modern highways or railroads? Are specific places that are noted in the travel accounts still identifiable on the landscape?

If students live in an urban area, the questions will involve changes in the urban landscape. What means of transportation were mentioned in the historic accounts? Do these means of transportation still exist, or have they changed? In what ways have neighborhoods been transformed? How has the city expanded? What kinds of city services were mentioned in the accounts, and have they changed? How has the ethnic composition of the city changed?

Increasingly, libraries and archives are digitizing historic materials, so travel accounts such as those described above may be available on local library or historical association web sites for many places. If such materials are not available locally, students could access more general accounts such as Lewis and Clark's journals (available on the PBS site at http://www.pbs.org/lewisandclark/archive/) or Oregon Trail pioneer accounts (available on the End of the Oregon Trail Interpretive Center site at http://www.teleport.com/~eotic/).

Accounts of trips to a foreign country abound on the Internet and may be located by looking under the country name. For example, a very interesting illustrated account of a trip to Mongolia titled "Greg's Mongolian Journal" appears at http://www.oz.net/guerrero/. Such accounts may be geographically naïve when compared with the reports of professional explorers or scientists, but they compensate in several ways. They are written in lay person's terms, which may make them more accessible for students. They reveal information about how people live, about how places look, and about the traveler's impressions, which may be left out of more formal reports.

First-person reports by survivors of natural disasters are also easy to locate on the Internet. They commonly appear soon after a hurricane, earthquake, tornado, volcanic eruption, or tsunami, for example. The Miami Museum of Science hurricane site at http://www.miamisci.org/hurricane has information for younger students that includes a family's account of surviving Hurricane Andrew in 1992. Another good hurricane site with activities for older students (6–8/9–12) is at Discovery.com (http://school.discovery.com/schoolfeatures/index.html). This site has excellent links to other hurricane-related web sites. First-person accounts of disasters reveal a great deal about the event itself and also may provide information on the reactions of official agencies and individuals to the crisis. For places that have the potential to suffer a particular type of natural disaster, for example, hurricanes on the Gulf or Atlantic Coast, or earthquakes in the western United States, first-person accounts may also be instructive for student disaster preparedness training. For some disasters that occur in non-English-speaking areas it may be difficult to locate survivor accounts in English. Hurricane Mitch, which impacted Central America in 1998, and the Sisani Lagoon tsunami of July 17, 1998, in the country of Papua New Guinea, are two recent examples where many newspaper accounts and other secondary sources are available but primary sources are hard to locate.

COLLECTING DATA FROM THE FIELD

Early geographers described the things they saw using their own observations or first-person accounts from others as the primary data source on which to base their descriptions. They relied on their own deductive ability to explain what they observed or read about. Typical of these early geographers were people like Charles-Marie de la Condamine and Alexander von Humboldt. De la Condamine was a French mathematician and scientist who led a seven-year expedition to South America between 1734 and 1741 to help determine the exact shape and dimensions of Earth. Von Humboldt was a German geographer who made an epic tour of the Americas between 1799 and 1804. Both of these men were part of the early effort to measure different physical characteristics of Earth and both were keen observers of the world around them. They recorded their observations and tried to develop rational explanations for what they found. The journals of geographers like de la Condamine and von Humboldt are still useful primary sources for learning what the places they visited were like at the time the reports were made. (A short biographical sketch of Alexander von Humboldt can be located on the Internet at the Geography Site at http://geography.tqn.com/library/weekly/aa020298.htm and information about Charles-Marie de la Condamine is on the History of Mathematics site at http://history.math.csusb.edu/Mathematicians/La_Condamine.html.)

The attempt to explain the world links modern geographers with their forebears of the Age of Enlightenment. They are still engaged in observing, explaining, and predicting. To do this they need many different kinds of data. These data come from an almost infinite variety of sources. Some geographers still collect data in the field just as de la Condamine and von Humboldt did. Students may follow this tradition by writing descriptions of the areas in which they live or through which they travel as they go to school, shopping, or on other trips through their community. Family vacations provide another possibility for students to keep a travel diary in which they record their observations as they travel to new places. When they do this, they are collecting their own primary source data. If they cannot conduct their own fieldwork, they may want to look at some of the virtual field trips on the Internet that are noted in Chapters 3 and 4.

Because modern technology has provided us with such an amazing variety of machines that help us to gather data, nowadays it is often not necessary for geographers to actually go into the field to obtain data for their studies. Geographers use information downloaded from satellites and ground sensors, or collected via censuses, questionnaires, or in a wide variety of other ways. These data sources have transformed our ability to observe and understand the processes, both natural and human induced, that are transforming Earth.

CENSUSES, STATISTICAL REPORTS, POLLS, AND SURVEYS

Human geographers are interested in how people live and how they interact with the environment in which they live. Much of the data that human geographers use comes from censuses, surveys, and statistical reports of one sort or another. A *census* is a periodic count of the population usually conducted by a national government. Censuses have been around for millennia but the first decennial (every decade) census was conducted in the United States in 1790. The United States has conducted a census every ten years since then in order to determine the distribution of population to insure equality of voting in accord with the Constitution. Addresses for United States census Internet sites are listed below and in Chapter 4.

Most censuses concentrate on counting noses—finding out how many people live in a place. However, they also collect information on a wide variety of other characteristics of population. Most censuses record data on age, gender, and marital/family status (is the head of household married, divorced, single; how many people live in a residence and what is their relationship to each other). The United States census also collects information on quality of housing, employment status and occupation as well as race and/or ethnic affiliation. In the United States, the population census is now conducted by mail, and census takers will visit only households from which a mail questionnaire is not returned. Other information may be collected via a *random sample* that is designed to obtain data from a representative group rather than the entire population of the United States.

Most other countries also conduct regular censuses but the period between censuses, the type of data collected, the method of collection, and the consistency of data collected from census to census all vary greatly. (See Chapter 3 for information on the Mexican census web site and Chapter 4 for the German and Indian censuses.) Some countries do not collect data on ethnic affiliation, others may not report certain kinds of economic information, and still others may add or delete certain information on health or educational status. All of this makes it difficult to compare censuses conducted by different national governments.

Another important issue with respect to censuses is accuracy. The United States, which has the longest continuous record of census taking and which uses very sophisticated techniques to insure the accuracy of its census, admits to a five percent error rate. To make matters worse, the error rate varies spatially and with respect to ethnic minorities. The census tends to be more complete in rural and suburban areas where middle-class families live and less accurate in inner cities and some rural areas where there may be people living in irregular circumstances. African Americans and Hispanics are more likely to be missed by the census than Caucasians. (Papers discussing census undercounts with special reference to ethnic minorities and recent immigrants are available on the Census web site at http://www.census.gov by clicking on estimates in the "people" category. Actual data comparing "official" and "estimated" results from the 1990 census are also available at this site at the Census 2000 prompt.)

Other countries, especially those undergoing civil unrest or suffering from other kinds of problems, are likely to have high rates of error. Usually the errors are undercounts, resulting from people being missed. Occasionally individuals may be assigned to an incorrect ethnic group or otherwise placed in a wrong category. Those who regularly use census data learn to spot discrepancies that may reveal an error, but some are subtle and may persist for years before anyone finds them.

Most national governments collect a variety of socio-economic data in addition to the demographic information that is the main focus of the national census. These data may provide information on literacy and education, health facilities and health status, sanitation conditions, housing, distribution of employment across sectors of the economy, economic activity by sector, imports and exports, and many other social and economic indicators. Some of these data are collected as part of national censuses, but much of it will be gathered from other sources. Often such data is summarized annually making it more current than census data.

The extent to which this data can be considered a primary source is debatable. Data are usually released in aggregated form, for the entire country or by state, province, or other major internal division. On the other hand, the published data are the least refined source that is generally available, so some would consider such information to constitute a primary source. Many countries have Internet sites on which such social and economic data may be accessed. It is also available from some international organizations such as the World Bank (http://www.worldbank.org).

Surveys and polls differ from censuses in several important ways. Usually they focus on a relatively narrow range of topics and they use a sample group rather than covering an entire population as a census does. Also, many polls tend to focus on topics related to marketing, politics, or economic issues and may be of marginal interest for geographers. Nevertheless, some poll data may be tabulated by region of the country and the differences among regions may reveal interesting clues to social or economic differences within the country. Some polls compare attitudes among different ethnic groups living in the United States, which likewise, is of interest to geographers. Another important aspect of surveys and polls is that they are often conducted by private organizations. The data they collect are geared toward the specific needs of the group for whom the survey is conducted and the data may not be released to the public except in summary form (i.e., the primary data are not available). Clearly, this limits the utility of polls and surveys. Still, a wide variety of poll data is available from certain web sites such as the Pew Center for the People and the Press (http://www.people-press.org/content.html) and the University of Michigan Inter-university Consortium for Political and Social Research (http://www.icpsr.umich.edu/). Not all of these polls deal with topics of interest to geographers, but some do.

SOURCES OF DATA ON ENVIRONMENTAL CONDITIONS

There are many different sources of information on environmental conditions on the Internet. Temperature and precipitation data by month, as indicated earlier in the case of Los Angeles, are available for all major cities of the United States. Data for many other parts of the world may be accessed at the World Climate site (http://www.worldclimate.com/) or for some countries through sites maintained by their meteorological service.

Other data on physical conditions are not as readily available on the Internet. Cloud cover, sea surface temperature, and other climate-related data are relayed to Earth from satellites on a regular basis and may be accessed at sites such as NOAA (http://www.nws.noaa.gov/climate.shtml), World Meteorological Organization (http://www.wmo.ch/), and the Lamont-Dougherty Geophysical Laboratory of Columbia University (http://ingrid.ldgo.columbia.edu/). Soil types and characteristics are problematic because the data are complex and the maps large scale, but they can be accessed for locations in the United States at the Department of Agriculture's Natural Resources Conservation System site (http://www.nrcs.usda.gov/index.html). A learning module for lower grade students on soil development is also available at this site, as is additional data on natural resources of the United States. Changes in vegetation cover can be observed from satellite images and other remote sensing sources via the United States Geological Survey at its Earthshots site that was previously noted.

MAPS

Sites such as the Perry-Castañeda Library of the University of Texas (http://www.lib.utexas.edu/Libs/PCL/Map_collection/Map_collection.html) and the Library of Congress (http://lcweb2.loc.gov/ammem/gmdhtml/gmdhome.html) have reproduced historic maps. However, the small size and relatively poor quality of reproduction of these maps limits their utility. Historic maps are also reproduced in web sites featuring historic events such as the Lewis and Clark route, cited earlier in this chapter.

Topographic maps are analyzed in some specific sites such as Topozone (http://www.topozone.com). They suffer from some of the same problems of scale and quality of reproduction as the historic maps. The United States Geological Survey maintains the "Finding Your Way with Map and Compass" site (http://mapping.usgs.gov/mac/isb/pubs/factsheets/fs07999.html), designed to teach students to use topographic maps to locate themselves.

Several web sites produce local street and road maps for virtually any place in the United States as well as for some foreign areas. These maps can be very useful for locating specific addresses, determining street patterns, and similar activities. For the United States, the Census Bureau's TIGER data base is useful (http://www.census.gov/geo/www/tiger/index.html), and private sources such as MapsOnUs (http://www.mapsonus.com), MapQuest (http://www.mapquest.com), and MapBlast (http://www.mapblast.com) also feature large-scale street maps.

GROUND-LEVEL PHOTOGRAPHS

Visual images are a strong point of the Internet. Web sites abound with interesting illustrations that show places in the United States and elsewhere in the world. These illustrations range from tourist photographs to significant historical photographs and drawings. "Greg's Mongolian Journal," cited above, contains photographs illustrating contemporary conditions in Mongolia, one of the world's most isolated countries. Tourist-oriented sites exhibiting professional and/or amateur photography exist for nearly every country in the world. The possibilities for developing exciting and challenging geography exercises are limited only by the imagination of the teacher. The Electronic Field Trip of Glacier National Park (http://www.sd5.k12.mt.us/glaciereft/home.htm)

has many photographs of cultural and physical features of this famous national park. An interesting critical thinking exercise using this site could ask students to prepare a diary describing their trip and commenting on each photograph.

AERIAL PHOTOGRAPHS AND
OTHER REMOTELY SENSED DATA SOURCES

Aerial photographs date from 1858, when a French photographer used a balloon as a platform to make photographs of Paris from above Earth's surface. The first documented aerial photographs in the United States were made of Boston in 1860. Shortly thereafter, cameras borne in balloons were used to monitor troop movements and other military activity during the Civil War. Modern satellite imagery has its origin in these early experiments with photography from a unique bird's eye perspective. For decades aerial photographs were made from airplanes on black and white film and variations in gray tones were used to interpret the resulting images. Today, in addition to images in the *visible spectrum* (color), a wide range of other radiation wave-lengths is used to derive images of Earth, other planets in the solar system, and distant stars, nebulae, galaxies, and other astronomical features. On Earth, infra-red sensors can detect heat loss from buildings, motorized military equipment such as tanks and armored personnel carriers, and surfaces of different temperatures. Such images have wide application in energy conservation, military intelligence, and climatology and meteorology, among other fields. Ultra-violet radiation is useful for evaluating certain vegetation types and for penetrating military camouflage. Sonar uses sound waves to map the ocean floor and for coastal navigation, and radar has been employed to map areas such as parts of the Amazon Basin that are often covered with clouds and invisible to sensors in the visible and near-visible bands of the *electromagnetic spectrum*.

An array of satellite images has been mounted at the University of Maryland Meteorology Department web site (www.meto.umd.edu/~owen/EARTHCAST/). Most of these images are intended to facilitate weather and climate analysis but some may be used for viewing other aspects of the physical earth, as well. Many United States government sites also provide satellite images that are designed for instructional uses. In addition to the USGS Earthshots site already noted, the National Aeronautics and Space Administration (NASA) also provides many satellite images at http://earth.jsc.nasa.gov/.

The Virtual Geography Department at http://www.utexas.edu/depts/grg/virtdept/contents.html, maintained by the University of Texas Department of Geography, links to an Aral Sea site that has many satellite and space shuttle images of the sea as well as surrounding areas of Central Asia. This site deals specifically with the reduction in area of the Aral Sea during the past thirty years as more and more water is taken for irrigation from the rivers that feed it. Some of the photography on this site is very impressive.

CONCLUSION

As the discussion above demonstrates, primary sources in geography cover an exceptionally diverse range of possibilities. In reality, any first-hand source that has spatial characteristics or that deals with environmental issues could be useful for helping students learn about geography. Critical thinking skills may be brought into play in the analysis of nearly all of these materials. Understanding and interpreting narrative, statistical, or visual data such as that described in this chapter requires that students be able to classify the materials, compare and contrast the critical elements in them, manipulate them, and draw conclusions about cause and effect from the data. Sequencing is called for in working with historical materials and problem-solving and decision-making are required in determining what information is relevant to a problem and in preparing reports.

With respect to the sites noted above, and the Internet in general, the usual caveats apply—sites vary greatly in quality, some data are aggregated in ways that reduce their utility for geographers, and some may contain errors or be presented in such a way as to lead to questions about their quality, lack of bias, or general usefulness as teaching/learning materials. We have tried to screen out the least useful sites and focus on ones that seem especially relevant. But the number of sites grows exponentially and there will be new areas of the Internet to explore, old sites will disappear or change their content, sites that are excellent now may become dated or lose their relevance, while sites we may have opted not to include may add important new data that increases their value. One should be constant in the search for new and better materials to use in the classroom.

REFERENCE

Dunn, Oliver, and James E. Kelley, Jr., trans. (1989) The *Diario* of Christopher Columbus's First Voyage to America 1492–1493. Abstracted by Fray Bartolomé de las Casas. Norman: University of Oklahoma Press.

Geographic Research, Geography Standards, Critical Thinking, and the Internet

3

As we have noted in the preceding chapters, geography is a highly diverse field. Thus, it should not be surprising to discover that geographical research is highly varied, both in its focus and its methods. This chapter will look at geographic research from the perspective of the world wide web, examining the kinds of research that may be found by exploring the Internet or that may be conducted using Internet resources.

RESEARCH IN GEOGRAPHY

Research is a word with many different meanings. At the most basic level, research consists simply of posing a question and locating the resources necessary to answer it. For geography this may be as simple as looking in an atlas, gazetteer, or encyclopedia to get information about a place and its location. However, for many scientific geographers, research involves framing their questions as hypotheses and ensuring that their results may be replicated by others. These geographers make use of the scientific method or some other conceptual framework to structure their investigations. For these more complex research problems one may have to resort to technical materials, raw data, or field work to obtain the information needed to find an answer.

For beginning students, research questions will be simple and straightforward and can probably be answered by referring to commonly available maps, data sources, and reference works, many of which may be available on the Internet. Students in higher grades may be expected to frame questions in the form of hypotheses and to utilize more sophisticated sources in seeking answers.

As the level of sophistication of questions increases, the likelihood that a straightforward answer will be found is reduced. Students will probably be called upon to use their own judgement to select among several alternate possibilities or to evaluate several options for finding the answer to a question or testing a hypothesis. Many Internet sites present data that may be used to develop geographically related hypotheses and/or provide information necessary to test them.

Answering all but the most simple research questions requires critical thinking. Students are called upon to refine their questions so they are meaningful and capable of being answered. They must evaluate a range of possible strategies or sources to locate an answer or test their hypotheses, and often they must discriminate among two or more possible answers. Geographic research may call upon students to read and interpret maps, manipulate and assess statistical data, read and evaluate written diaries and other historical records, or extract information from photographs and other graphic materials. Sometimes students can conduct their own fieldwork or simulate it in virtual field trips on the Internet, making maps from their own observations and data collection, conducting interviews, or gathering and/or locating population or other numerical data. All of these activities employ critical thinking skills.

The sites reviewed in this chapter fall into one of several categories. Some are sites that present the results of research conducted by a practicing scientist. Such sites provide examples of application of the scientific method or a similar scientific research strategy to the solution of a real-world problem. Other sites contain case studies that present a scenario and ask students to consider different approaches to addressing the issue in question. Virtual field trips are popular on the Internet. Such sites provide students with an opportunity to experience vicariously a visit to a physical area to which they would not normally have access. Virtual field trips pose questions that can be answered by students based on the visual material included within the site. Finally, some of the sites discussed below contain raw data that may be used by students to construct maps, tables, or graphs that help them pose hypotheses or develop theories related to the topic with which they are working.

The discussion of research that follows is laid out to follow the six essential elements around which the national geography standards are organized: (1) The World in Spatial Terms; (2) Places and Regions; (3) Physical Systems; (4) Human Systems; (5) Environment and Society; and (6) Uses of Geography. This organizational framework is repeated in Chapter 4 with exercises keyed to specific sites in the context of the essential elements.

MAPS AND SPATIAL RELATIONSHIPS

The first element of the national geography standards focuses on examining relationships among different phenomena on Earth's surface. Maps are one of the most useful tools for learning about spatial relationships on Earth. Maps are also geographers' special tool and the one with which they are most associated. Geographers use maps to record data, to interpret landscapes, and to detect change. Learning to read and interpret maps is a fundamental geography skill, as is the ability to make sketch maps from raw data. Maps are a fundamental tool for understanding *spatial relationships*—where things are in relationship to each other on Earth's surface. For students, learning to read maps and using that information to draw inferences about spatial relations is an important critical thinking skill. The National Atlas of Canada site (http://atlas.gc.ca/) has an excellent introduction to maps with examples of many of the different types of maps discussed below. To access the map section click on the "teaching resources" prompt then go to "Carto Corner."

Maps come in many different forms but geographers often divide them into two broad classes based on their content. Base maps are used for non-specialized purposes such as teaching or locating countries, rivers, mountain ranges, bays and seas, and similar features. Base maps include the physical/political maps that are commonly used in classrooms and also topographic maps that are produced by government agencies in various countries for use by campers and hikers, surveyors, and the military. These maps show a wide range of information about the form of the land and the features humans have built, but they do not include specialized data. For that, one needs thematic maps. Thematic maps are intended to show a specific distribution. Thematic maps in atlases, for example, show production of certain crops, distribution of population and demographic features, economic characteristics, and many other specific social, economic, health, and demographic characteristics of the world and its subregions. The most commonly used maps are physical/political maps, mainly because of their utility in the classroom, but thematic maps are generally more useful for geographic research.

Base Maps and Geographic Research

Base maps help geographers locate places and see the relationships that exist among different features of Earth's surface. Where are the world's major mountain ranges, rivers, seas, and lowlands? How do these basic physical characteristics relate to the world's political units?

Africa provides an excellent theater for research on the relationship between physical features and political boundaries. For example, students may look at a physical/political map of the country of Tanzania (many other African countries would do as well for this exercise) and observe the country's boundaries (there are many sources for country maps such as Atlas of the World at http://cliffie.nosc.mil/~NATLAS/ index.html). What observation can be made about Tanzania's international boundaries? Students should note that Tanzania's northern boundaries are straight lines while the others are irregular and they should develop hypotheses to account for these two types of boundary lines. Then they can use the map to locate information to support or refute the hypotheses. If they have trouble developing hypotheses they can access "The Geography Page" at http://www.rev.net/~aloe/geography/ and click on "explanation and comparison of theories" to see many different ways of setting boundaries. For Tanzania the northern boundaries were surveyed between certain physical features such as the shore of Lake Victoria and Mt. Kilimanjaro, while the irregular boundaries generally follow physical features such as the center of Lake Tanganyika, the shore of Lake Malawi, the Great Rift Valley, and the Ruvuma River. From this information students can develop general hypotheses about the nature of political boundaries and test them using other maps.

Topographic Maps

Topographic maps are large-scale base maps that show elevation and landform features using contours, shaded relief, hypsometric divisions, hachuring, or some combination of these techniques. A skilled map reader can use a topographic map to find out what kinds of landforms are shown on the map and from this infer the geological processes which produced the landscape depicted. *Cultural features* such as roads, railroads, towns and cities, and rural settlements are also shown in topographic maps, so they reveal information about how humans have modified the landscape and about relationships between human activities and *physical features*. Topographic maps are often used as base maps for hikers, hunters, orienteers, and others who need to have a large-scale map that accurately represents the landscape of a fairly small area. Most topographic maps in the United States are produced at a scale of 1:24,000 (2 5/8 inches represent 1 mile). In most of the rest of the world maps are produced in the metric system and use a scale of 1:50,000 (2 cm represent 1 km). Topographic maps are also commonly produced at smaller scales such as 1:100,000, 1:250,000, and 1:1,000,000, but maps at these scales eliminate so much detail that they have limited value for most outdoors activities. *Aeronautical charts*, used by pilots to identify landmarks, identify airports, and plot a course using visual references, are specialized topographic maps with useful features for pilots to use in orienting themselves. They are usually published at a smaller scale than standard topographic base maps 1:1,000,000 (an example of an aeronautical chart may be found on Carto Corner at http://atlas.gc.ca/english/carto/map9.html).

Topographic maps are produced for the United States by the United States Geological Survey (http://mapping.usgs.gov/). Most foreign countries have a similar mapping agency that provides large-scale maps of the national territory. Canada's national mapping agency is the Centre for Topographic Information (http://maps.nrcan.gc.ca). Mexico's Instituto Nacional de Estadística Geografía e Informática (INEGI) is responsible for making topographic maps of the national territory, collecting social and economic data, administering the national census, collecting and selling satellite imagery, aerial photography, and similar kinds of data (http://www.inegi.gob.mx/). The United Kingdom's Ordinance Survey is one of the outstanding map publishers in the world, producing a wide variety of maps for use by clients who range from professional surveyors to tourists (http://www.ordsvy.gov.uk/). Australian's Surveying and Land Information agency produces topographic maps of that country (http://www.auslig.gov.au/) and New Zealand's National Topographic/Hydrographic Agency produces maps of its territory (http://www.linz.govt.nz/index.html).

Topographic *contour maps* use contours, or lines that connect points at the same elevation, to show differences in elevation. These maps lend themselves to many different types of research. They may be used to examine the relationships between settlements and landforms; they are useful for discovering patterns in transportation routes, city layout, drainage (i.e., stream systems), geographic names (which may reveal a great deal about the history of a place), and a multitude of other geographic elements. A good site to find contour maps is the TopoZone site (http://www.topozone.com). Students can look up the town where they live on this site, which has topographic contour maps for the entire country. Other examples of contour maps are available at the Library of Congress site "Mapping the National Parks" (http://memory.loc.gov/ammem/gmdhtml/nphtml/nphome.html). Contour maps, shaded relief maps, and combined contour/shaded relief maps of national parks are on the Perry-Castañeda Library web site at: http://www.lib.utexas.edu/libs/PCL/Map_collection/National_parks.

Similar to topographic contour maps, *shaded relief maps* also may be used to interpret the kinds of landforms that characterize an area. Shaded relief maps indicate landforms by using shading to represent shadows as if the light were coming from one side of the map. This allows the cartographer to depict the shape of landforms in such a way that an experienced map reader can tell what kinds of geologic processes shaped the map area. Shaded relief maps are included in many national park web sites such as Rocky Mountain National Park where contour and shaded relief maps of the same area may be compared by clicking on "Historic USGS Maps" in the Rocky Mountain National Park Virtual Tour web site, which was developed by the United States Geological Survey (http://rockyweb.cr.usgs.gov/rmnp/). Shaded relief maps of the fifty states are available via the Color Landform Atlas of the United States at Johns Hopkins University (http://fermi.jhuapl.edu/states/states.html).

Hypsometric maps use colors to indicate different elevations (see Carto Corner at http://atlas.gc.ca/english/carto/map.5.html or the Atlas of Lane County http://geography.uoregon.edu/infographics/lcweb/lcindex.htm for examples of hypsometric maps). This technique is generally used on small-scale maps such as physical/political maps intended for school use. Low elevations are usually indicated by green tints, with higher elevations grading into yellows and browns. This color scheme has the advantage of representing elevations in familiar earth tones. On the other hand, there is a tendency for users of hypsometric maps to confuse the green and brown colors with climate, instead of elevation, thus attributing high precipitation to some desert lowlands and likewise, assuming that the humid eastern slopes of the Andes Mountains of South America, for example, are dry, when the brown tint used to represent them actually reflects their elevation.

Hachure maps are rarely seen now, but the technique was popular, especially in Europe, during the nineteenth century and the first decades of the twentieth century. Hachure maps employ fine inked lines to represent landform features. Mountains, for example, are shown by short parallel lines drawn up and down the slope across the contour. An example of a hachure map may be found on the Mt. Rainier Centennial web site of the National Park Service (http://www.nps.gov/features/mora_cenn/map3.htm). This map portrays the northwest coast of North America and also has a large scale view of Mt. Rainier which shows hachures very clearly.

Thematic Maps

Thematic maps present data on specific topics. The kinds of information that may be presented on thematic maps is limited only by the imagination of the person who compiles them. Population distribution maps show the distribution of population for the world or for a smaller area. If the objective is to show the concentration of population in different parts of the world, a dot map in which an individual dot on the map represents a certain number of people is preferred. A *cartogram*, in which countries or other commonly recognizable areas are drawn in proportion to the size of their population, would be effective for comparing the population of different areas. Cartograms may be used similarly to compare other quantitative values such as social or economic data. Social and economic data such as gross national or domestic product per capita, levels of urbanization, literacy, life expectancy, and a wide range of other such data may also be shown on a *choropleth map*, which uses patterns or colors to represent categories of values. These maps allow for easy comparison of statistical data among countries or regions. For an example of a choropleth map see the Arizona Population Change map on the EPA site at http://www.epa.gov/ceisweb1/ceishome/atlas/stateatlas/arizona_pop_chan.htm. Students could locate data to create their own maps or interpret existing maps that they find on the Internet.

INEGI, cited above, maintains a bilingual Spanish/English web site that contains current information on Mexico's population and economy (http://www.inegi.gob.mx/). Mexican population data are presented by state on the INEGI homepage. Click on the "statistics" prompt, then click on "socio-demographic aspects" and, finally, "population by state." Students who access this web site could develop a system for making a choropleth map of Mexican population by state. To make a choropleth map students will have to determine a logical set of population size categories into which to divide the population data and then assign each category an appropriate pattern or color symbol. The number of categories along with the population limits for each should be developed by the students. The complete map is an example of a thematic map—in this case, Mexican population by state. Students might look at other maps in the INEGI site, such as transportation (railroads and highways) and precipitation, to see if there are any associations with population. This exercise will involve students in classifying, problem-solving and decision-making, and, possibly, cause and effect.

Mental Maps

Mental maps are the images of the world we carry in our mind. Mental maps may be images of familiar places such as our home neighborhood, places we visit frequently, or places we have never visited but know only from images we have seen on television, in books or magazines, or through other secondary sources. For familiar places, mental maps reflect the landscape features of which we are aware but omit features that fail to attract our attention. These mental maps affect the way we visualize the world in which we live and they also influence the travel routes we select, businesses we frequent, and our perceptions of areas as positive, negative, or neutral. For areas with which we may not be familiar, mental maps help to shape our vision of the world. Do we know if a place is located in the tropics or temperate zone? Is it on a seacoast, in the mountains, or crossed by a great river? Do the people speak English or another language? How do they earn a living, what religion do they practice, and what kinds of food do they eat? Is our image of the place positive or negative? Would we like to visit there? Is it a place in which we would feel safe and secure or is it filled with danger? Is it beautiful or ugly, polluted or pristine, familiar or alien?

The mental maps we carry about places are shaped in large part by the media to which we are exposed. To the extent that all the citizens of a country or region are exposed to the same information, there are shared images of places. These images, in turn, can influence travel, trade, and even our national foreign policy.

Students could test their mental maps of local places by drawing sketch maps of their neighborhood and comparing them with street maps from the Internet. Street maps are available from many different sites such as MapsOnUs (http://www.MapsOnUs.com), MapQuest (http://www.mapquest.com), or MapBlast (http://www.mapblast.com). Students may be surprised at how far off their mental maps are from the actual street grid of their neighborhood. To add an element of critical thinking to the exercise, students can consider reasons why their mental maps deviate from physical reality.

For unfamiliar places, students can be asked to write down their images of a country or place. They then can search the Internet for web sites that contain maps, descriptions of location and physical characteristics, statistical data, and photographs of the area and its people. Students may compare what they learn from the Internet with their initial mental map of the place.

These elements of spatial analysis make up a fundamental aspect of geographic research. Our physical and mental maps shape the way we see the world but they also provide fundamental information we use to determine how the different elements of our landscape relate to each other.

THE DISTINCTIVE CHARACTER OF PLACES AND REGIONS

Places are described and differentiated on the basis of their physical and cultural characteristics. Regions are classified on the basis of these characteristics, as well, and regions are the fundamental units of organization for our world.

Some Internet sites contain traditional *regional geography* information on landforms, climate, ethnic groups, and economy. Kenya has a particularly attractive regional site named Kenya—Our Land that provides a detailed look at each of the country's eight provinces and forty-five districts (http://www.kenyaweb.com/ourland/ourland.html). A regional research project could involve students identifying the most suitable district in which to place a certain economic activity such as a fishing cooperative, a logging operation, a pineapple plantation, or a cattle ranch.

Students would utilize information from the site to prepare a report that would support their choice of location for the activity.

The Department of Geography at the University of Edinburgh maintains web sites on the city, Tour of Edinburgh (http://www.geo.ed.ac.uk/home/tour/edintour.html) and on Scotland, Scotland Tour (http://www.geo.ed.ac.uk/home/scotland/scotland.html). The Scotland site offers a wide range of possibilities for research in regional geography. Students may learn about physical geography as well as Scottish history, Scots Gaelic language, local government, the new Scottish parliament, and Scotland's place within the United Kingdom. Some questions that could stimulate research include: Is Scotland a country? How are Scots different from British? What is the United Kingdom? Why is Scotland's climate so mild?

The Edinburgh site offers a virtual tour of the city along with comparisons of Edinburgh's climate with areas of similar climate elsewhere in the world. The site is loaded with possibilities for comparative research with other parts of the United Kingdom as well as with other parts of the world. For example, students might compare Edinburgh with a comparably sized city in the United States or Canada.

Regions and places derive their special character from the interaction of *physical and cultural characteristics* that has taken place there. The Internet offers many opportunities to share vicariously the adventures of travelers to exotic places. An example is a tour of a Costa Rican rainforest on the Ecofuture web site at http://www.ecofuture.org/ecofuture/pk/pkar9512.html. The illustrated tour vividly describes the sights, sounds, and feel of a walk through a tropical rainforest. A research component could involve students finding out more about the animals described in the tour or learning more about tropical rainforests and why there is so much concern for their preservation. Key words to use include biodiversity, climate change, deforestation, and tropical ecology.

The Persian Gulf area is a region that is of intense interest in the United States because it has been the site of recent political conflict and because the Persian Gulf states control over half the world's proven oil reserves. Columbia University has developed a special Internet site that focuses on the Persian Gulf countries, The Gulf 2000 Project (http://Gulf2000.columbia.edu/). This site provides a brief introduction to the region and dozens of links to information on the eight Persian Gulf States (Bahrain, Iran, Iraq, Kuwait, Oman, Qatar, Saudi Arabia, and the United Arab Emirates). The number of links varies somewhat with the country—larger countries such as Iran and Iraq have more sites available while the smaller countries are less well covered. Nevertheless, the Gulf 2000 Project is an excellent place to begin a research project on the geography, economy, cultures, or other aspects of any of the countries in the Persian Gulf region.

The characteristics of places are often evoked by literature and in art and photographs. Mark Twain is one of America's greatest writers. A large part of his writing includes colorful descriptions of places Twain knew or had visited. He grew up in Hannibal, Missouri, and some of his most colorful descriptive writing is set in Hannibal or along the Mississippi River. In 1875 Twain wrote a series of seven short articles which he titled "Old Times on the Mississippi" for *Atlantic Monthly Magazine*. These texts have been reproduced at the About.Com Mark Twain site (http://marktwain.about.com/library/guides/bl_guide_lm01.htm?pid= 2734&cob=home). Students can conduct research on sense of place by reading one of Mark Twain's "Old Times on the Mississippi" sketches and commenting on what it tells them about Missouri and the Mississippi River in the mid-nineteenth century. More ambitious students might want to search for sites with descriptions of Hannibal and the central Mississippi River as they are today. Information is available on the Hannibal home page at http://hanmo.com/hannhom3.html. Students might be asked to explore the question, How is being the birthplace of a famous writer reflected in modern Hannibal, Missouri?

William Faulkner was another well-known American writer whose work is even more grounded in a regional landscape than Twain's. The University of Mississippi maintains a web site, William Faulkner in Oxford, Mississippi, that compares Faulkner's fictional Yoknapatawpha County with his actual home town, Oxford, Mississippi, the county seat of Lafayette County (http://www.mcsr.olemiss.edu/~egjbp/faulkner/ wftown.html). Oxford and Lafayette County were models for the places described in Faulkner's literature. Students can conduct research using this web site and its links to examine how an author uses local geography and sense of place to create a fictional world. Specific questions that might be asked include: How did Faulkner "create" a place? What physical and cultural elements are illustrated in the web site? How much does the fictional Yoknapatawpha County actually resemble the real Lafayette County, Mississippi?

LANDFORMS, CLIMATE, VEGETATION, AND OTHER PHYSICAL SYSTEMS

Physical geographers ask questions about the physical world in which we live. What is the distribution of precipitation around the world and what seasonal patterns may be observed? Where are the mountains, lowlands, upland plateaus, and other distinctive landforms of Earth? What is the pattern of distribution of these characteristics and how is this related to theories of the structure of Earth? What are the global or regional patterns of vegetation and to what extent are they linked to climate and soil distributions?

NOAA, the National Oceanic and Atmospheric Administration of the United States, through its GLOBE Program, encourages students to collect a range of environmental data, report the data to the national center via the Internet, and formulate research problems that use the data they and students at schools around the world have contributed. This research-based program has great potential to help students learn more about the physical world. The program may be accessed at http://www.globe.gov/fsl/welcome.html?lang=en&nav=1. The GLOBE Program is somewhat different from other sites we have discussed because the Internet is the coordinating mechanism and the data are collected by students themselves. Teachers and students should be prepared to become links in a world-wide, continuing program. If they do so, students become directly involved in research on physical processes and environmental change.

The Science Learning Network (http://www.sln.org) is a site that provides links to museum web sites around the country. The Oceans Alive site is an excellent introduction to the 70 percent of Earth that is covered by water. This site, maintained by the Museum of Science in Boston, has pages on the topography of the ocean basins, *plate tectonics*, ocean currents, ocean-atmosphere interaction, and several other aspects of the physical geography of the oceans. Links to other ocean-related sites are also provided. This site affords many opportunities for students to conduct their own research. For example, the tide page provides instructions on collecting tide data and using it to predict lunar cycles; the ocean current page describes experiments to determine the effect of temperature and salinity on water density and to demonstrate the circular motion of ocean waves. The Science Learning Network also provides a link to Earthforce and El Niño sites from the Franklin Museum of Science in Philadelphia that deal with dynamic processes in Earth and the atmosphere. Earthforce provides information on volcanoes, earthquakes, tsunamis, glaciers, avalanches, and floods. There are many links to related sites on the Internet as well. El Niño focuses on Earth-atmosphere relationships and on the role of El Niño in shaping the world's weather. The site also includes a simple experiment to demonstrate the effect of water temperature on the atmosphere. This site provides dozens of links to other El Niño sites, opening many possibilities for students to expand their research beyond the Franklin Museum site.

Glacier National Park Virtual Field Trip (http://www.utexas.edu/depts/grg/virtdept/contents.html) provides students with an opportunity to learn about glacial processes and landforms, wildlife, and map reading. The exercise is complete with maps, student questions, and other supports. The virtual field trip requires downloading of PDF files and may not be accessible to some systems.

Virtual Tour of Mendenhall Glacier (http://www.snowcrest.net/

geography/field/mendenhall/ index.html) is a related site that allows students to take a trip by air over an Alaskan glacier. The tour is accompanied by explanations of *glaciation processes* and study questions that will stimulate students to process the information they acquire from the photographs and maps.

Several other virtual field trips are available on the Virtual Geography Department page from the Department of Geography at the University of Texas at Austin (http://www.utexas.edu/depts/grg/virtdept/ contents.html). This site is a work in progress and frequent stops should provide a flow of new trips.

CULTURE AND ECONOMY: HUMAN SYSTEMS

The activities humans carry out on the land comprise a bewildering array of options. We all must earn a living somehow, but the ways in which this is done vary tremendously from place to place, as do our ways of communicating with each other, our forms of worship, and nearly every other element of human culture. Many countries have web sites that may be accessed to provide students with an overview of national culture and economy. Many of these sites are oriented toward promoting tourism and they must be viewed with some caution because they tend to focus on the more attractive aspects of a country. Nevertheless, such sites may be used to gain an idea of what life is like around the world.

Malaysia has developed one of many sites to showcase national culture. Titled simply Malaysia, this site (http://www.interknowledge.com/ malaysia/main.html) includes information on national parks, archaeological sites, history, urban centers, tourism, and national culture. Students can conduct research on Malaysia using this site. Questions they could answer include those involving national history, ethnic groups, major cities, religion, and tourist attractions. Why does Malaysia have so many ethnic groups? What cultural differences are there in the different areas of the country (i.e., Malay Peninsula, Sarawak and Sabah)? Since the site is tourism-oriented, students could browse the pages on national parks to plan a tour itinerary for Malaysia. They might also conduct research on the different cultural and religious traditions (Hindu, Moslem, Buddhist, Christian) that have influenced the area and relate these to larger patterns of migration through history.

The Department of Geography at the University of Wisconsin Eau Claire posts student and faculty research projects on its web site, Geography Department Showcase (http://www.uwec.edu/Academic/ Geography/showcase.htm). These research projects will change from time to time but they represent the application of scientific principles to analysis of problems in human and physical geography. In Fall 1999 the research on the site included a student project on the Washington, D.C. Metro system and its relationship to retail development. This is an excellent example of research in human geography.

HUMANS INTERACTING WITH THE ENVIRONMENT

Many of the sites referred to previously in this chapter deal with human relations with the environment. This section focuses mainly on sites that are specifically related to contemporary ecological issues, especially as they relate to air and water pollution, global warming, geologic hazards, and similar phenomena.

The Virtual Tour of Rocky Mountain Park, cited earlier in this chapter (http://rockyweb.cr.usgs.gov/rmnp/), includes two case studies of landscape change, a lightning-caused forest fire, and a flood that resulted from collapse of an artificial dam. Both sites include comparative before-and-after maps and photographs along with explanatory text. The Ouzel Fire site provides an opportunity for students to evaluate fire policy in national parks. Burning and fire control policy became very controversial after the 1988 fires in Yellowstone National Park. The past and current policies and reasons for them are described on the Yellowstone National Park web site at (http://www.nps.gov/yell/nature/fire/wildfire.htm). This topic is one where students could debate the pros and cons of fire suppression and controlled burning policies based on information from the sites noted above. An alternative research topic could be to have students locate other web sites on the use of fire as a forest management strategy.

The Lawn Lake flood in Rocky Mountain National Park was caused by failure of a dam on the Roaring River. The flood caused substantial damage in the downstream community of Estes Park, Colorado and destroyed riverbank forests. While the Lawn Lake flood was a relatively small event, it represents a more serious potential problem with dams. The Teton Dam failed in 1982, flooding Rexburg, Idaho and smaller towns downstream. This flood is chronicled on two web sites, Teton Flood Museum (http://www.rexcc.com/museum.htm) and Teton Flood (http://www.ida.net/users/elaine/idgenweb/flood.htm). These sites and the events they describe draw attention to the issue of flood plain development and problems of old and/or structurally unsound dams. Such dams pose serious danger for people who live downstream. Students could search for sites related to other dam failures (Johnstown, Pennsylvania, 1889, for example; see the Johnstown Flood National Memorial site at http://www.nps.gov/jofl/home.htm) or look for information on intentional dam removal for a variety of reasons (see, for example, the Columbia and Snake Rivers Campaign web site at http://www.columbia-snake.org/).

Salton: A Sea of Controversy (http://ublib.buffalo.edu/libraries/projects/cases/salton.html) is a case study intended to introduce students to issues of human modification of the environment. The Salton Sea was created when the Colorado River breached its banks in 1905, flooding a depression in the Imperial Valley of California. The sea is now a runoff catchment for irrigation water and agricultural chemicals from nearby farming areas. The case study deals with public responses to the pollution of this man-made salt lake and presents some strategies that are being considered for alleviating the problems. Students are asked to answer a series of study questions after reviewing the materials in the case study.

The Petition: A Global Warming Case Study (http://ublib.buffalo.edu/libraries/projects/cases/petition.html) is a case study that evaluates responses to concerns about global warming by considering both sides of the controversy. It presents arguments for and against controlling greenhouse gas emissions and also introduces ethical questions about methods used by supporters and opponents of proposed international treaties on global warming. The case study ends with four questions for students to consider. Students could conduct their own research on this topic by locating Internet sites dealing with global warming and assessing them for their perspective—what point of view do the sites seem to favor: (1) global warming is a problem of human origin that must be addressed immediately, or (2) the origins of climate change are poorly understood and may be the result of natural processes rather than human actions, thus no radical action is called for at present with respect to greenhouse gas emissions.

The St. Lawrence Seaway opened in 1959. The Seaway is a system of canals, locks, rivers, and lakes that connects Great Lakes ports in Canada and the United States with the Atlantic Ocean. The Seaway has fostered the development of trade and industry in the Great Lakes. It is also a major feat of engineering. The Great Lakes/St. Lawrence Seaway System home page is at http://www.seaway.ca. The site is bilingual in English and French, but most users in the United States will probably prefer to click on the English prompt for the English language version. Information on these pages includes an interactive map of the Seaway, data on lock specifications and other engineering details, statistics and graphs on cargo types, and a list that compares the Seaway travel distance to points in Europe with those from other ports in North America. There are also links to web sites for several major ports in the system that contain interesting information on facilities and cargoes.

This site lends itself to research on several topics. Students could conduct research comparing various ports in the Seaway system on the basis of facilities or type and tonnage of cargo. The data on shipping could be plotted on a map that would allow easy comparison among ports. In another project students could look for comparative information on other lock and canal systems. The Zonian Site (http://www.zonian.com/index.html) contains very good information on the Panama Canal, including an animated illustration of the operation of locks complete with photos of ships passing through the Canal. The New York State Canal System web page (http://www.canals.state.ny.us/) has information on four New York canals, including the historic Erie Canal.

GEOGRAPHY APPLIED TO PRACTICAL PROBLEMS

Geography is a very practical discipline. Geographers are concerned with scale, or the size of the area in which they work. At the smallest scale geographers look at the entire world or large world regions. At this scale they are involved in analyzing international trade, global climate change, vegetation change, population distribution, water availability for deserts and semi-arid areas, and a wide variety of other global-level issues. At the national level geographers help to draft regional plans for resource development, land use, transportation development, and many other national government planning efforts. At the local level, geographers work as city planners, marketing specialists, and real estate developers. All of these activities are based upon research.

At the regional scale in the United States, The New Deal Network (http://newdeal.feri.org/), sponsored by the Franklin and Eleanor Roosevelt Institute and the Institute for Learning of the Teachers College/Columbia University, has a very useful site that contains a wealth of information on the Tennessee Valley Authority (TVA). The TVA is an autonomous governmental organization charged with development of the Tennessee River Valley. The TVA was created during the great depression of the 1930s and continues to provide electricity service, flood control, recreation opportunities, development assistance, and research on a wide range of power-related and other social and economic issues. TVA was responsible for transforming the geography of the Tennessee River Basin. The Authority built dams, constructed roads, transformed farming techniques and crops, provided electricity to rural dwellers, and opened long stretches of the Tennessee River and its tributaries to navigation. The New Deal Network site provides information on the TVA and the geographic and social transformations for which it was responsible.

To access the TVA pages from the New Deal Network home page, click on "TVA: Electricity for All" at the prompt. This will take the viewer into a TVA page that opens to seventeen other pages and several lesson plans. The pages labeled "People of the Norris Basin" and "Changing the Land" are the most relevant for geography. Students can access these pages to see how people lived in the Tennessee Valley before the TVA was created and learn how TVA transformed people's lives and the landscape. Students should look for changes in the regional farm economy, including land use, standards of living, and changes in housing. While the TVA was generally considered to be a very successful government-sponsored development program, there were negative impacts for some. Students should consider the plight of people who were displaced from their homes by dam projects and the reaction to TVA by private power companies and other entities that were threatened by the competition. A research component might involve students accessing the official TVA site (http://www.tva.gov) to discover how the TVA operates today. The power generation pages provide information that allows students to compare the relative benefits of coal-fired, hydroelectric, and nuclear power generation.

Nunavut is a newly created Canadian territory that is controlled by the Inuit (Eskimo) people. The territory is huge, covering some 733,000 square miles or nearly the size of Mexico. The population of this great land is only about 22,000, which makes it one of the emptiest areas in the world. The new capital, Iqaluit (formerly Frobisher Bay), is located in the southern part of Baffin Island and only a few miles south of the Arctic Circle.

The people of Nunavut are planning to develop the region along sustainable principles. Students can learn about Nunavut by accessing Nunavut Handbook at http://www.arctictravel.com/. This site provides current information on Nunavut, including regional and town maps, descriptions of parks and nature reserves, economic development plans, and other data on the new territory. Students might use this site to plan a trip to Nunavut, investigate business opportunities, or assess the long-term prospects for economic viability of the territory.

For trip planning students should review the site to determine what tourism possibilities exist and decide what they would prefer to do from among the various options. For example, they could see a polar bear, go cross-country skiing, fish in Hudson Bay, look at wildflowers in the tundra, see examples of native arts and crafts, learn native crafts, or go kayaking. Then they should use the web site to select the best destinations and times of year to visit Nunavut for the activity they have chosen. As an extension of this exercise students could use the Internet to plan their travel from home to the destination they have chosen in Nunavut.

Moving from one environmental extreme to another, coral reefs are among the world's most diverse ecosystems. The Great Barrier Reef of Australia is the world's longest reef. The reef is a protected area, most of which lies within Great Barrier Reef Marine Park. The Australian government maintains a web site that provides information on the park's unique life forms and the efforts being made to protect them (http://www.gbrmpa.gov.au/). This site explains how the government of Australia, through the Great Barrier Reef Marine Park Authority, is attempting to resolve the multiple demands on the park by fisherfolk, tourists, and residents of the nearby coastal areas. The park managers also must cope with changing public attitudes about the role of the park and nature conservation in general. Basic research for students might involve visiting the site and considering the various points raised in the park authority chair's comments on managing the park. The students could then debate the various issues raised in the article, taking the role of someone in the fishing economy, a tour boat operator, a marine biologist, and the park manager to discuss strategies for resolving the potential conflicts. Then they could respond to the question, What could a geographer contribute to the debate about use of Great Barrier Reef Marine Park? As an extension of this exercise students could locate web sites on the Belize Barrier Reef, the second longest in the world, to compare conservation efforts there with those of Australia (start at http://www.belizenet.com/, Belize by Naturalight, which is a general home page for the country). One clear difference between the two countries is that only small parts of the Belize Barrier Reef are in protected areas such as parks.

The Ice Age Floods Institute of Moses Lake, Washington, a private non-governmental organization, maintains a web site on the great Lake Missoula flood of 12,000 years ago which shaped the current landscape of much of the inland Pacific Northwest (http://www.uidaho.edu/igs/iafi/iafihome.html). The site includes a map and a brief explanation of the causes and impacts of the flood. The Ice Age Floods Institute is promoting development of a parkway that would link flood-related sites of interest in a four-state area (Idaho, Montana, Oregon, and Washington). This is an interesting example of how private groups lobby for development of natural areas with tourist potential (a similar site that promotes transportation development is the Bering Strait Tunnel site at http://www.arctic.net/~snnr/tunnel/intro.html).

At the local level, the British Ordinance Survey has a web site that offers an excellent introduction to applied geography research (http://www.ordsvy.gov.uk/). The British government is trying to reduce traffic congestion around schools. One of the strategies they have developed involves getting parents to let children who live close to schools walk rather than taking them in a car, as is currently done. Sustrans is a program to locate and mark off safe walking routes for school children. Students may access the Sustrans site by logging onto the Ordinance Survey site and clicking "Education" on the menu on the left side of the window. A second click on "Introduction" will bring up the Sustrans information. Students can obtain street maps of the area around their school from one of several web sites such as MapsOnUs (http://www.MapsOnUs.com), MapQuest (http://www.mapquest.com), or MapBlast (http://www.mapblast.com) and use these as a base for laying out safe walking routes for their school using the criteria indicated in the Sustrans web site.

CONCLUSION

The sites noted in this chapter are well-adapted to student research projects. However, they hardly scratch the surface of what is available on the Internet, where there are literally hundreds of sites that are related to geography in some way and offer possibilities for developing critical thinking skills through research. In Chapter 4 we will offer suggestions for evaluating Internet sites. We will then examine additional sites and suggest extended inquiry-based activities that may guide student research. The possibilities for research using the Internet are almost without limit when students employ a creative combination of innovative search techniques and critical thinking skills.

Utilizing Internet Sources to Promote Critical Thinking in Geography

4

Earlier chapters have established the place of primary sources and critical thinking in the exercise of the discipline of geography. A goal of geography education is to cultivate in young learners those habits of thinking that define the practitioner of geography. Geographers value first-hand observation and data collection as they conduct research to augment their understanding of Earth and its many dynamic and complex, inter-related systems. Ideally students would travel to the site of study to observe and gather primary data from which to draw conclusions about the world and its people. Realistically, this is not possible. However, students can draw upon primary sources compiled by others. Such sources include statistical databases, maps, oblique and aerial photographs, satellite images, and first-person written accounts, to name but a few. Access to primary source materials allows students to analyze and interpret data for themselves, evaluate information, and arrive at conclusions on their own. In other words, students begin to exercise the skills and apply the habits of mind that professional geographers employ in their pursuit of knowledge.

TRANSLATING INFORMATION INTO KNOWLEDGE

Primary sources, in whatever form, are nothing more than an accumulation of information until the researcher—student or professional—applies the skills of critical thinking and thereby transforms that information into knowledge. Students who acquire knowledge through the filter of a teacher's or textbook author's perspective have been denied the true experience of learning. Primary sources, because they generally involve "raw" data that has not been processed or interpreted, require thoughtful inspection, analysis, and decision-making on the part of the student. The skills of critical thinking—questioning, reflection, association, hypothesizing, generalizing—place the student at the center of the learning process. As a result, the student is empowered to take charge of his or her own learning and is more likely to transfer critical thinking skills to other arenas of learning involving secondary sources. Students are less likely to accept information as knowledge. Students are better equipped to deal with the problem-solving demands of the real world.

The study of geography is a key element of every student's basic education. Geography provides the context within which issues of concern in today's complex world occur. Geography also provides an excellent environment within which students can practice and cultivate skills of critical thinking, skills which are essential to finding solutions to problems facing the world at scales ranging from local to global. Geography's focus on dynamic data and processes and its concern with issues of place and space make the use of critical thinking in association with primary data pivotal to knowledge formation.

The Internet has opened the door to a whole new realm of opportunity for students seeking primary source materials to support their research. Resources previously limited to the libraries of major research institutions are increasingly available with just a few clicks on the keyboard. Consequently, students are turning increasingly to the Internet for answers to questions. Ease of access does not, however, come without risks. Volume does not equate to value. Not all information available on the Internet is reliable or without bias. As a result, students (and teachers, as well) must learn to evaluate each site before accepting the information that is presented. In other words students must exercise skills of critical thinking as they access various sites before they even begin to analyze the data that is presented. They need to raise questions about the reliability of the source of information, any bias that may be inherent in the presentation of information on the site, the comparability of the data available, and finally the appropriateness of the data for the purposes of their research. In short, they need to ask, How do I know that this is true? Will the information available on this site serve my research objectives? How can I evaluate this site?

EVALUATING INTERNET SITES

While the Internet opens countless doors to information, it lacks the quality assurance filters traditionally provided by librarians or peer review of print resources. As a result the burden of validation generally falls to the researcher. When the researcher is a student, who may have limited experience or knowledge of the topic, critical evaluation of Internet sites is essential. Since a typical search may yield dozens, even hundreds of seemingly promising sites, some basic guidelines for sorting out reliable sources can be helpful.

- Affiliation—A reliable Internet site will have a clearly identified author or organizational affiliation. In addition it will provide contact information other than just an e-mail address, such as a phone number or mailing address. A reliable site will invite inquiries or suggestions. Such sites frequently provide a link to the main site of the parent organization or institution. Another clue to affiliation is found in the site address itself. Sites that provide statistical or other factual data compiled by an educational institution or government agency frequently have an address that ends with **.edu** or **.gov**. Sites for groups or organizations that may represent a particular point of view often have an address that ends with **.org**. Finally, sites representing some commercial interest usually have an address that ends with **.com**. While not a foolproof test, critical attention to address endings can provide important insight into a site's purpose.

- Bias—Students must be alert for signs of potential bias or for advocacy of a particular point of view. Bias may be detected in the form of direct statements, but it may also be more subtle, as in the omission of certain types of information or points of view. Generally, if the author or affiliation is clearly identified, the potential for bias is more apparent. Students need to be especially cautious in evaluating sites without clear authorship since such sites may be promoting a particular slant on the topic. Students should not necessarily avoid sites that present biased information; they just need to approach such sites with open eyes and a critical mind so that they do not mistake one perspective for total objective truth.

- Clarity—An Internet site that has numerous spelling or grammatical errors should be approached with caution. At the very least, such errors suggest low quality control standards that may carry over into the accuracy of information provided. At worst, such errors reflect a disregard for accuracy and scholarly detail. A site should be easy to navigate and any graphics should be clearly labeled and easy to read. Lack of attention to such details again suggests poor quality control.

- Documentation—It is especially important that information presented on an Internet site be as carefully documented as that published in traditional print sources. A reliable site provides the user with the sources of information and statistics included, and frequently includes links to original sources of data. Good documentation allows the user to confirm the accuracy and completeness of the information presented. In addition to documentation of the source of information, a good Internet site includes the date of the latest update. This is a critical piece of information since it reflects on the currency of material included on the site. In a discipline like geography this is especially important since much of the data dealt with is dynamic. For example, undated demographic or economic data is of little value and can even be misleading since both types of data are subject to almost constant change. Students should develop the habit of questioning sources and timeliness of data.

Application of these A–B–C–D guidelines in order to evaluate Internet sites critically requires both patience and practice. The guidelines are organized in an easy-to-remember alphabetical format: affiliation, bias, clarity, and documentation. A site which scores high in all of these categories is likely to be reliable. One which falls short on one or more should be evaluated with a certain degree of skepticism. Exercised carefully, these guidelines represent an important part of developing critical thinking skills in the context of successful Internet use.

USING PRIMARY SOURCES FROM THE INTERNET

The remainder of this chapter is devoted to identifying sites that include primary source materials available via the Internet. Sites have been selected for their reliability, their general freedom from built in bias, and their appropriateness and adaptability for use by students. The relevance or geographic context of each topic and data set, as well as a brief description of the site, is followed by questions and activities that involve students directly in the process of learning. Students are encouraged to apply the critical thinking skills of questioning, analyzing, and evaluating in order to arrive at conclusions on their own. As a result of direct experience with primary data, students not only improve their thinking skills, but also expand their content knowledge.

The sites that follow are organized loosely around a framework derived from *Geography for Life: National Geography Standards, 1994.* (For an online tutorial to *Geography for Life*, see the National Council for Geographic Education at http://www.ncge.org/tutorial/introduction.html.) Many of the sites are cross-cutting and can easily be related to more than one essential element or standard. Each activity is adaptable for use as a focal point for a class assignment or as an individual research project. Although the questions and activities target the middle high school years, they are adaptable for use with classes ranging from middle school through the final year of high school or even early college.

While every attempt has been made to select sites for which addresses are unlikely to change, the Internet is dynamic. As a result many sites may change over time and some sites may require new addresses or even disappear. Should this occur, you may be able to locate the desired information by the careful use of key words and one of the many available search engines.

RESOURCES FROM THE INTERNET

Almost any topic can have a geographic perspective; it is just a matter of posing the right questions. The concepts and questions suggested in previous chapters can be applied to many sites that are rich in primary sources that provide information that can become the basis of knowledge formation if approached with a critical eye. No attempt has been made to provide an exhaustive list; Internet sites are too fluid to make that possible. Instead, representative examples are identified that can be used as a foundation for building one's own list of favorite sites.

"Geography studies relationships between people, places, and environments by mapping information about them in a spatial context" (*Geography for Life* 1994: 34). This involves several skills:

- the ability to describe where groups of people, places, and different physical environments are on Earth, to see how they relate to each other in space, and to explain why they are located where they are.
- the capacity to identify a pattern of spatial organization by observing the distributional characteristics of individual objects, that is, are the objects clustered or scattered, are they oriented with respect to some physical or cultural feature (rivers, bays, valleys, transportation hubs, mines, zones of agricultural production, etc.)?
- the capability to use concepts such as location, distance, direction, density, and form to visualize the relationships between elements of the landscape in a designated area or region.
- the insight required to use maps, data, and other sources of information on physical and human characteristics of the landscape to find the proper questions to ask in order to explain the patterns that have been identified through the processes noted above.

1. MICROSOFT TERRASERVER

Site address: http://terraserver.microsoft.com

Type of data: aerial photographs; satellite images

Key terms: remotely sensed image; natural and cultural landscape; physical and human characteristics of place

GEOGRAPHIC CONTEXT

Access to *remotely sensed images* (images collected from above Earth's surface) has afforded geographers an entirely new perspective on the planet we call home. The ability to view places from above allows observations of patterns and relationships that are often less obvious from a ground-level perspective. Aerial photographs capture a landscape at a given moment in time, preserving both human and physical characteristics of place for comparison and analysis with either earlier images or current observations. "TerraServer" is a database of images for much of the United States and Europe as well as selected other locations. Images may be accessed by clicking on an interactive map or by entering either a place name or an absolute location (latitude and longitude coordinates).

THINKING CRITICALLY

1. Use "TerraServer's" search function to locate an image of the area surrounding the school or some other site of local interest. Zoom in to a level that allows identification of details of the *natural and cultural landscape*. Note the date and scale of the photograph. Prepare a sketch map of the area visible in the photograph for comparison with current landscape characteristics of the area.

2. Use images from "TerraServer" to plan a field trip in the local area. During the field trip, keep careful notes about observations of *physical and human characteristics*. Then compare your field notes with the aerial photographs. Prepare a class presentation in which you point out and account for differences discovered.

3. Using "TerraServer's" search function, enter the coordinates 39°N, 77°W. This is an image of Washington, D.C. Use the navigation and zoom functions to locate the Mall, the popular tourist area that extends from the Capitol building to the Lincoln Memorial. Compare the photograph with a map of the same area. Use a debate format to argue the advantages and disadvantages of these two ways of representing an area.

4. Use "TerraServer's" search function to locate aerial photographs of several major cities in the United States and Canada. Observe characteristics shared by all cities and characteristics that seem to be limited to only one or a few cities. Prepare a poster that illustrates characteristics of all urban places. Lead a class discussion to explore the questions, Do most cities share certain common characteristics? To what extent are these characteristics visible in your town? Why? Why not?

2. THE ELECTRONIC MAP LIBRARY

Site address: http://130.166.124.2/library.html

Type of data: thematic maps

Key terms: graduated point symbols; population distribution; racial/ethnic groups; socio-economic indicators

GEOGRAPHIC CONTEXT

Thematic maps present data in a direct, readily understood format. While thematic maps are selective in what they present, showing only one or a few data sets, or "themes," and omitting large amounts of additional detail, they do have the advantage of showing the selected data in terms of volume or amount in a spatial context, or, in other words, where the selected phenomenon occurs in space, in relation to other examples of that phenomenon. The "Electronic Map Library" includes digital atlases of selected major metropolitan areas of the United States. Each atlas includes a variety of maps based upon demographic data sets, such as population and race, income, poverty, and education. Maps employ color and *graduated point symbols* (symbols of proportional size reflecting different ranges of data values) to represent the data.

THINKING CRITICALLY

1. Select the "San Francisco Bay Area Atlas." Then select "Population and Race"; then select the map of "Total Population 1990." Note the distribution of total population in the metropolitan area. Now select the maps for various racial and ethnic groups that make up the San Francisco population, for example non-Hispanic white; Hispanic; Black; Asian. Note the patterns in distribution of the various groups. Locate physical and political maps of the San Francisco area and speculate on factors that may influence the patterns in *population distribution*, for example mountains, wetlands, access to water, transportation lines.

2. Select atlases for several cities, for example Boston, Chicago, and San Diego. Then select "Population and Race" and compare the composition of the population in each city. Conduct research in order to script a role-play activity in which representatives of various *racial/ethnic groups* explain how they came to live in each city.

3. Select atlases for San Francisco and Los Angeles. Then select "Population and Race"; then select the maps for total population. Compare the distribution patterns of population in each city. In what ways are they similar? In what ways are they different? Brainstorm factors that might account for such patterns. How old is each city? What role might time of origin play in the evolution of spatial patterns? (Hint: think about modes of transportation.)

4. Select the "Seattle, Washington and Vicinity Atlas" (or that of any other metropolitan area). Select maps for population, income, and educational attainment. Compare patterns and distributions among the various groups that make up the total population. Based on your observations, frame a set of generalizations about the relationships among these *socio-economic indicators*. Then develop a set of questions that you can use to test your generalizations.

3. U.S. CENSUS BUREAU: "TIGER MAPPING SERVICE"

Site address: http://tiger.census.gov

Type of data: digital map database

Key terms: spatial relationships; scale; data classification

GEOGRAPHIC CONTEXT

Maps are the tools most commonly associated with the practice of geography and maps represent the geographer's most effective tool for showing *spatial relationships,* or the association between or among phenomena on Earth. The TIGER Mapping Service enables on-line mapping of selected data from the U.S. Census, thus allowing observation and analysis of patterns and relationships. The site supports representation of social and economic data at a variety of scales for any location in the United States.

THINKING CRITICALLY

From the "TIGER Mapping Service" main page:

1. Select "The TIGER home page." Scroll down almost to the bottom of the page and select "TIGER Map Service" for on-line mapping. The default map screen shows a map of the District of Columbia and surrounding areas of Maryland and Virginia. Use this default map to practice using the tools of TIGER mapping. For example, use the buttons in the upper right corner of the window to zoom in or out on the map. Note how the map scale (shown in the key below the map) changes as you zoom in or out. How does *scale,* or degree of generalization, affect the representation of data? Use the boxes to the right of the map to turn map layers on or off. For example, turn off the layer showing "parks," then "redraw" the map. How might the absence of this layer affect your analysis of population distribution? Scroll down below the map. Under "Map Census Statistics," select from the drop-down menus a data level and a data theme. For example, you might select "census tract" and "family income." Note that you also choose the method by which data will be classified, that is, by quintiles or equal intervals. Draw the map using each method and compare the result. What are some advantages and disadvantages of each *data classification* method?

2. Select "The TIGER home page." Scroll down almost to the bottom of the page and select "TIGER Map Service" for on-line mapping. Scroll to the bottom of the default map page and select "United States." Under "Map Census Statistics" choose from the drop-down menus "state level" and "% Hispanic." Also select "quintiles." Then "redraw" the map. In a short essay describe the distribution pattern of the Hispanic population in the United States. Speculate on factors contributing to this pattern. Identify ways in which you could test your hypotheses.

3. Select "The TIGER home page." Scroll down almost to the bottom of the page and select "TIGER Map Service" for on-line mapping. Scroll to the bottom of the default map page and select "Northeast U.S." Under "Map Census Statistics" choose from the drop-down menus "Congressional district level" and "% Age 65+." Also select "quintiles." Then "redraw" the map. Describe the patterns in the distribution of the elderly population in the northeast United

States. What effect might this pattern have on voting patterns in these states? Assume you are a congressional candidate from southwest Pennsylvania running against an incumbent candidate. Draft an agenda of key issues for your campaign.

4. Select "The TIGER home page." Scroll down almost to the bottom of the page and select "TIGER Map Service" for on-line mapping. Scroll to the bottom of the default map page and enter in the Search box the name of a town or city in your state. Develop a series of maps that present data at different scales. Then lead a class discussion to analyze the patterns and relationships that you can observe on the maps. Summarize your analysis in an essay.

Additional online mapping site:

U.S. Geological Survey "National Atlas of the United States" (3a)

http://www.nationalatlas.gov/

"The identities and lives of individuals and peoples are rooted in particular places and in those human constructs called regions" (*Geography for Life* 1994: 34). Places and regions are central to geographic understanding in that:

- each place on Earth is distinguished by a unique combination of physical and human properties that set it apart from all other places. Learning to observe, record, and classify such properties is the first step in honing a geographic perspective on the world.
- regions are geographers' way of bringing order to Earth's incredible diversity. Regions exist only as people define them. A region is an area that possesses uniformity in terms of one or more criteria chosen to define it, such as wheat production in the region known as the Wheat Belt.

4. THE LIVING EDENS: VIRTUAL TRAVEL

Site address: http://www.pbs.org/edens/

Type of data: field notes; photographs

Key concepts: physical characteristics; natural environment; interaction

GEOGRAPHIC CONTEXT

Sights and sounds enhance the learning experience in ways that textbook readings can never equal. When students learn to use their eyes and ears to explore distant places, they begin to practice the art of thinking geographically. "Living Edens," based on the Public Broadcasting System television series by the same name, opens the door to distant places through photography and personal accounts of observations and experiences.

THINKING CRITICALLY

Open the "Living Edens" site and scroll down to the "Previous Sites" drop-down menu.

1. Select "Madagascar—A World Apart." Then select "Notes from the Field." Read the excerpts from the field journal of film producers Andrew Young and Susan Todd. View Madagascar through their eyes and make a list of all the *physical characteristics* of place that they mention in their field journal. Then

classify the items recorded in terms of land, water, atmospheric, and biotic phenomena. Based on its location (18°05'S, 43°12'E), what type of environment would you expect Madagascar to have? Are these physical characteristics typical of such an environment? Why? Why not?

2. Select "Bhutan: The Last Shangri-la." Examine the photographs of Bhutan's natural environment and wildlife in "Land of the Thunder Dragon" and "Animal Archive." Use the photographs to develop a descriptive profile of the *natural environment* of Bhutan, then evaluate the narrative included with the photographs. Have the authors presented an accurate description of this remote Himalayan kingdom?

3. Select "Namib: Africa's Burning Shore." Read cinematographer Richard Matthews' account of the Namib in "Recalling Namib." What challenges did he face? Put yourself in his place and plan a trip to the Namib. What supplies would you need? Look at the photographs in "24 Hours in Namib." Write your own account of a trip across the Namib. What might you see?

4. Select "Manu: Peru's Hidden Rainforest." Visit the people of the Yura Indian community living in Peru's Manu National Park through the pages of film producer Kim MacQuarrie's 1989 journal. Use MacQuarrie's observations to profile this remote group of people. What is their world like? How do they live? What do they eat? What challenges do they face each day? What evidence of *interaction* with the outside world did MacQuarrie observe? What changes do you think MacQuarrie's visit may have introduced? Select "The People of Manu" to read anthropologist Glenn Shepard's description of the native people of Manu. Compare his description to the profile you developed based on MacQuarrie's journal.

Alternative virtual travel site:

Travel to Antarctica, deserts around the world, and the country of Ethiopia through online passages from literary works. (4a)

http://www.envirolink.org/oneworld/tfocusc.htm

5. VIRTUALLY HAWAII

Site address: http://www.satlab.hawaii.edu/space/hawaii

Type of data: ground and aerial photographs

Key concepts: physical characteristics; cultural landscape

GEOGRAPHIC CONTEXT

Direct field observation is the geographer's preferred means to gather information and learn about Earth. However, travel to distant places is often not an option for students. Virtual field trips, such a "Virtually Hawaii," bring far-away places into the student's domain and allow observation, comparison, and analysis. Photographs, both ground-level and aerial, capture moments in time and allow students to hone skills of observation and remote data collection.

THINKING CRITICALLY

On the main page of "Virtually Hawaii," select "Take a Virtual Field Trip."

1. Select the island of "Oahu." Use the images of Oahu to create a narrative profile of the *physical characteristics* of this island. Then select the island of Hawaii, known as the "Big Island," and compare the physical characteristics of this larger, younger island with those of Oahu. Prepare a list of generalizations about features of volcanic landscapes. How can this list be tested?

2. Select the island of "Maui." You have the option of viewing selected places on Maui from the air or from the ground. Move quickly through first the air photographs and then the ground-level photographs. What are some advantages and disadvantages of each type of photograph for getting to know a place? Examine closely the images for aerial site #5 and ground-level site #10. Compare each perspective of the Haleakala Volcano. Prepare an illustrated report on the natural environment of this volcano.

3. Select the island of "Oahu." Select the "Walking Tour of Honolulu." The state of Hawaii is marked by its ethnically diverse population. Work through the walking tour of Honolulu, the state capital and largest city. Carefully read the *cultural landscape* and record observations in a field diary. Use your notes to write an essay describing the influence of various immigrant groups on the city's cultural landscape.

4. Select the "Big Island," then select "Kilauea Volcano." Take the "Radar Tour of Kilauea Crater." Make observations of physical and human characteristics of this active volcanic landscape. Visit another volcano site (for example, [15/16] http://www.geo.mtu.edu/volcanoes/) and compare the landscape of Kilauea with that of other active volcanoes. What generalizations can be derived?

6. JAPAN INFORMATION NETWORK: JAPAN ATLAS

Site address: http://www.jinjapan.org
Type of data: maps; photographs; interviews; data sets
Key terms: characteristics of place; aging population; population pyramid

GEOGRAPHIC CONTEXT

Japan is a major player in today's global economy. But Japan is an Eastern country, with its own unique set of values and attitudes. In order for the United States to interact successfully with Japan in the global arena, it is important that we understand Japan as the country sees itself. Through maps and photographs this atlas presents both traditional and modern images of Japan and the social trends that are shaping the country's future. The *Japan Atlas* is a product of the "Japan Information Network."

THINKING CRITICALLY

On the main page of the "Japan Information Network," select the "Japan Atlas."

1. From the "Index by Region," select the "Kanto Region." This is the region surrounding Japan's largest urban center, Tokyo-Yokohama. Examine the points of interest in and around this major city, as presented by the Japan Information Network. Compare this presentation of the Kanto region to that of one of the major urban areas of the United States, for example New York City, Los Angeles, or Chicago. What *characteristics of place* do these cities share? How is each unique? What biases or filters might the "Japan Information Network" have imposed on its presentation of the Kanto region? What biases may influence your perceptions of U.S. cities?

2. From the "Index by Region," select the "Kinki Region." Scroll down to "Architecture" and select "Historic Monuments of Ancient Kyoto." Kyoto is Japan's historical capital and center of traditional culture. Examine the photographs of Kyoto. What *characteristics of place* do these images reveal? Scroll to the bottom of the page and select "The 17 properties of World Heritage." Read about these World Heritage sites and compile a list of shared characteristics. Based on the information you have gathered, form a hypothesis about the role of tradition in Japan. How can you test this hypothesis?

3. On the main page of the "Japan Information Network," scroll to "Japan Insight" and select "aging society." Read the profiles (A–D) of Japanese senior citizens and identify some of the issues facing both the people and the country as the population ages. Compare the issues related to Japan's *aging population* (i.e., increasing median age) to those facing the aging population of the United States. Script a role-play in which a 70-year-old person from Japan talks with a 70-year-old person from your town about issues related to aging.

4. On the main page of the "Japan Information Network," select "Statistics." Then select "Census of Japan" and "Population (5-year age groups) as of 1999." Use this data to construct a *population pyramid* (a graph showing the distribution of the population by age and sex) of Japan's population. Then compare Japan's pyramid to that of the United States ([6a] http://www. census.gov). What similarities and differences do you observe? How do you account for these?

7. PALESTINIAN CENTRAL BUREAU OF STATISTICS

Site address: http://www.pcbs.org
Type of data: statistical data sets
Key terms: population pyramid; age structure; migration; quality of life

GEOGRAPHIC CONTEXT

National census reports often do not include data on refugee populations. As a result these groups are not accounted for nor are they included in national planning. When this happens, these "shadow" populations are left without a voice in decision-making processes that may influence their well-being and their political future. Nevertheless, these people are very much a part of the human face of the places in which they live. One such group is the Palestinians, a stateless group living in several countries of Southwest Asia (Middle East). The Palestinian Central Bureau of Statistics (PCBS) is the official source for statistics about the Palestinian people.

THINKING CRITICALLY

Open "Selected Statistics" on the "PCBS" main page.

1. Select "Demographic Survey," then "Current Main Indicators." The narrative that follows reflects the results of interviews conducted in the West Bank and Gaza Strip in 1995. Convert the statistical results presented in the narrative into a series of graphs that depict current demographic patterns among Palestinian households.

2. Select "Demographic Survey," then select the "1995" detailed statistics. Select "De Jure Residents by Age, Sex and Region–1995." Construct *population pyramids* (graphs showing the distribution of the population by age and sex) for the West Bank and Gaza Strip. Analyze the *age structure* (proportion of males and females in each age category) of these Palestinian populations, then compare these pyramids to that of neighboring Israel ([38] http://www.census.gov/ipc/www/idbnew.html). Write a news brief in which you compare the populations of Palestinian areas and Israel and speculate on reasons for the patterns in each pyramid.

3. Select "Demographic Survey," then select "1995" detailed statistics, then select "Relatives abroad by Country of Destination and Region–1995." Because of poor living conditions and lack of opportunity many Palestinians have migrated to other places. On a world map, show the distribution of Palestinians in other countries or regions. Select one of the destinations and write a letter to your cousin in the Gaza Strip describing your *migration* experience and your life in your new home.

4. Speculate on the effect of political uncertainty on *quality of life* in the Palestinian territories. Select "Area Statistics," then select "Housing Conditions," then "Annual Statistics." Examine the trend in various social indicators for 1995, 1996, and 1997. For example, look at average number of persons per room, connection to public sewer, access to flush toilet, and possession of a private car. What do these indicators suggest about quality of life in the Palestinian territories? Research such indicators for other countries. How do the Palestin-

ian territories compare? Write a position paper in the voice of a Palestinian representative speaking to the United Nations General Assembly.

8. AFRICA SPEAKS: STUDENT VOICES FROM AFRICA

Site address: http://www.uic.edu/classes/engl/engl161-patstoll/afspeaks.htm

Type of data: first-person accounts

Key terms: values/attitudes; cultural diffusion

GEOGRAPHIC CONTEXT

First-person accounts offer a learning opportunity that can never be achieved through secondary readings that impose the filter of the author's perspective or biases between the original source and the learner. Much of Africa remains shrouded in misinformation and stereotype. Nevertheless, understanding this region is a critical part of global education. Africa has the fastest growing population in the world but at the same time, much of this population lives in poverty. In order to find sustainable solutions to many of the region's problems, it is important to see Africa through the eyes of the African people themselves. This site records personal statements from African students in Niger, collected by a visiting American professor.

THINKING CRITICALLY

1. On the main page of the site "Africa Speaks," select "Customs 1" and "Customs 2." Read these passages written by college students from the University of Niamey in Niger. Identify similarities and differences between *values and attitudes* in Niger and the United States. What factors might account for these similarities and differences in cultural patterns? Is the culture of Niger more or less static than that of the United States? Why? Why not? What examples of *cultural diffusion* (the spread of an idea or culture trait from the center of origin) are evident?

2. On the main page of the site "Africa Speaks," select "Town and Country 2." Read the passages written by students at the University of Niamey in Niger in which they discuss life in towns and rural villages. What differences between town and rural life do they describe? What are some concerns they express? Conduct interviews to gather first-hand information about life in urban and rural areas of the United States. Are there similarities to the African accounts?

3. On the main page of the site "Africa Speaks," select "Letters Home." Read these letters of students to family members living back in traditional villages. What examples of change and conflict of values are revealed in these letters? How do you account for such issues? What role does education play in cul-

tural change? What role does living in an urban setting play in cultural change? Compare the experiences of these students in Niger to experiences of American students away at college. Write a letter to a relative explaining why you no longer agree with a particular custom or value that is shared by your family.

4. On the main page of the site "Africa Speaks," select "Politics 1" and "Trouble 1." Read these passages to identify issues facing the people of Niger. Make a list of problems and classify them according to type, for example, political, economic, environmental. Evaluate each problem to determine the cause. Is it the result of natural processes? Is it the result of human actions? Select one issue and prepare a development plan to address the problem. Keep in mind such factors as culture, resources, human resources, and cost. Present the plan to the class for their assessment.

9. TERRAQUEST: VIRTUAL JOURNEYS TO REMOTE LOCATIONS

Site address: http://www.terraquest.com/index.html

Type of data: photographs; maps; narrative; table

Key terms: Antarctic Treaty; Galapagos Islands; ecosystem; tourism; sustainability

GEOGRAPHIC CONTEXT

Each place on Earth is unique, but not each place is equally accessible. Some of the most interesting places are far away and difficult to visit except by virtual travel. Largely sheltered from the influences of cultural diffusion and change, these special locations retain a picture of life much as it was before the days of global exchange. Terraquest opens a window on such places for virtual travelers through photographs, personal accounts, and journals.

THINKING CRITICALLY

1. On the "Terraquest" main page, select " Going South—Way South." Enter the web site and select "Ship's Log." Select "Digital Daily" and read selections from the log. Compare passages written by different people on the same day, describing the same experience. Do people see a shared experience in the same way? Why? Why not? Take a walk with a friend. Each of you write down what you saw and felt during the walk. Then compare notes. What is the result?

2. On the "Terraquest" main page, select "Going South—Way South." Enter the web site and select "History." Then select "Antarctic Treaty." Read the main terms of the treaty. Do you agree with the treaty as presented? Research the

current status of the treaty? What changes have been proposed? Form your own position and write an editorial about the future of Antarctica.

3. On the "Terraquest" main page, select "Head for Virtual Galapagos." Make a virtual trip to the Galapagos Islands by viewing the photographs in "Photo Gallery" and "QTVR Gallery." Make notes about all you observe, for example, physical features, plant life, and unique living creatures. Then, from the main page navigate to the "Atlas" section on "Geology" and to the section on "Wildlife" to learn more about the things you have seen.

4. On the "Terraquest" main page, select "Head for Virtual Galapagos." Then select "Issues." What are some of the issues facing the fragile *ecosystem* of the Galapagos Islands? Which of these issues are related to human activity on the islands? Access the Galapagos web site through the link under the Charles Darwin Research Station ([9a] http://www.darwinfoundation.org). Access the "Site Map" and scroll down to "Tourists Visiting Galapagos, 1979–1997." *Tourism* is an important source of income for the islands. Construct a graph using the data in the table. In light of the issues facing the islands, is this level of tourism *sustainable*? Are the economic gains worth the environmental price? Decide where you stand on this question and write a convincing editorial supporting your position.

Additional virtual field trip site:

"The Nunavut Handbook" (9b)

http://www.arctic-travel.com

10. CITIES/BUILDINGS ARCHIVE: URBAN LANDSCAPES

Site address: http://www.washington.edu/ark2/

Type of data: photographs

Key terms: built landscape; culture traits; diffusion; human characteristics of place

GEOGRAPHIC CONTEXT

The *built landscape* is a reflection of people's response to and use of the environment in which they live. The built landscape can be read like the pages of a book to identify unique *culture traits* and influences of *diffusion* (spread of ideas). When first hand observation is not possible, photographs provide a window through which *human characteristics of place* can be noted. This archive of images from the University of Washington presents urban landscapes and building designs from countries around the world.

THINKING CRITICALLY

1. "Enter the archive." Select "Tibet." Then work through the photographs from Lhasa, taking notes in a journal as if you were on a field trip to this remote city. What do your observe about the physical landscape? What distinctive characteristics do you note in the built landscape? What difference do you note between town and rural images?

2. From the archive, select "Japan." Survey the photographs of buildings in Japan. Compare and contrast buildings that reflect traditional and modern styles. Why do you think modern buildings are so different? What geographic factors might account for modern building styles in Japan? What does this suggest about human characteristics of place?

3. From the archive, select "Austria." Take a virtual field trip through Austria by looking at each image and noting building styles and human use of the land. Select "India." Repeat the process of looking at each image and noting building styles and human use of the land. Select five images from each country that include specific examples from the built landscape which highlight basic cultural differences in these two places. Prepare a class presentation that explains the use of observations of the built landscape in order to understand unique culture traits of a particular place.

4. From the archive, select "Egypt." Examine carefully each photograph under the subject "old city." Assume you are a tour guide. Lead the class on a virtual field trip through this old section of Cairo, pointing out details of the built landscape that offer insight into the human geography of this place.

11. CIA ATLAS OF THE MIDDLE EAST

Site address: http://www.lib.utexas.edu/Libs/PCL/Map_collection/middle_east.html

Type of data: thematic maps

Key terms: region; patterns; physical environment; distribution; rate of increase; resource; human welfare

GEOGRAPHIC CONTEXT

Southwest Asia and eastern North Africa, commonly referred to as the Middle East, is a pivotal *region* (an area with uniformity in terms of one or more selected criteria) in terms of world politics and the global economy. A region of sharp contrasts, the Middle East has been plagued by conflicts rooted in culture, religion, scarce water resources, and economic disparities. Although thematic maps are selective in what they present, they can, if read critically, support comparison and analysis. The "Atlas of the Middle East" is a publication of the U.S. Central Intelligence

Agency and is one of many map collections available through the University of Texas "Perry-Castañeda Library" site.

THINKING CRITICALLY

On the "Maps of the Middle East" page of the "Perry-Castañeda Library Map Collection" site, select "Atlas of the Middle East."

1. Compare "Land Use" maps of several countries, for example, Bahrain, Egypt, Iraq, and Saudi Arabia. What *patterns* of land use can be observed? What patterns are common to all countries? Why? What patterns are limited to only some countries? Why? In what ways has the *physical environment* limited people's opportunities in this region? How might this be a source of tension or even conflict?

2. Compare "Population Density" maps of several countries. Is the population evenly distributed? Why? Why not? What patterns or associations can be observed in the *distribution* of population concentrations? Research the *rate of increase* of population in these countries (see the International Database of the U.S. Census Bureau at [38] http://www.census.gov/ipc/www/idbnew.html). How might the distribution patterns and rates of increase contribute to tensions in the region?

3. Compare "Economic Activity" maps of several countries in the region. Construct a chart that compares the main activities in the selected countries. What activities are common to most or all countries? What activities are limited to only some countries? What role does *resource* distribution play in the distribution of wealth and *human welfare* in this region? Write a position paper in which you propose a plan for economic assistance within the region to benefit those countries that have only limited resources. Present and defend your plan to the class.

4. Select the "Occupied Territories Map." Identify those territories that are in dispute in the region. Select "Country Information" to obtain basic physical, human, and political facts about these territories. Then select specific maps for the "Gaza Strip," the "Golan Heights," and the "West Bank." Read the maps to develop a profile of land use, population distribution, and economic activities for each territory. Debate the positions of both sides in each of these disputed territories.

12. THE SOUTH: WHERE IS IT? WHAT IS IT?: PERCEPTUAL REGIONS

Site address: http://xroads.virginia.edu/~DRBR/Reed/index.html

Type of data: thematic maps

Key terms: region; perceptual region; stereotype

GEOGRAPHIC CONTEXT

Geographers use *regions* (areas that are uniform in terms of one or more selected criteria) to bring order to a world of many different and complex phenomena. Regions are mental constructs that are generally classified as formal, functional, or perceptual. *Perceptual regions* are subjective, reflecting shared, but often difficult to measure understandings of place. They may be areas that everyone understands but that are very difficult to delimit on a map. One such region is the "South." On this site, John Shelton Reed uses an essay and maps from his book, *My Tears Spoiled My Aim*, in an attempt to answer the question, Where and what is the South?

THINKING CRITICALLY

1. Brainstorm a list of ten criteria to answer the question, Where and what is the South? Write a two or three sentence rationale for each criterion selected and identify the data that would be needed to measure or present the criterion. Debate the usefulness of the criteria chosen.

2. Open the site noted above. Examine the criteria used by Reed in his attempt to "find" the South. Compare his list of criteria to that brainstormed in #1, above. Classify Reed's criteria based on the type of information used. For example, the criteria might be sorted as political, historical, cultural, economic, and environmental.

3. Develop a set of questions to guide the evaluation of criteria used to define a perceptual region. Open Figure 1: "Percentage Who Say Each State Is Southern, 'All in All.'" Critique the map and the source of data on which it is based. Is this map based on fact or opinion? Select four more maps from the site and critique these? What role does *stereotype* play in Reed's choice of criteria? What role did stereotype play in your choices from his list? Write a carefully reasoned essay in which you define and evaluate the usefulness of perceptual regions as valid expressions of geography.

4. Identify other perceptual regions at either the local or national scale. Prepare and administer a survey among a cross-section of the local population to determine their mental map of the focus region. Be sure to consider what defining criteria you want to use. How might choice of criteria influence the survey outcome? Map and analyze the results of the survey. Consider the extent to which people's perceptions are objective or subjective.

"Physical processes shape Earth's surface and interact with plant and animal life to create, sustain, and modify ecosystems" (*Geography for Life*, 1994: 34). Physical processes, those acts of nature absent from human influence, play an essential role in all life on Earth because:

- Earth's physical systems—land, water, atmosphere, and living things—are individually and collectively affected by processes of creation, modification, and destruction that constantly change Earth's environment.
- physical processes act on Earth's systems in ways that create a wide range of opportunities and limitations within which people make choices based on their cultures and perceptions.

13. RIVERS SEEN FROM SPACE

Site address: http://www.athenapub.com/

Type of data: satellite and aerial photographs

Key terms: natural systems; floodplains; aerial photograph; false color; remotely sensed image

GEOGRAPHIC CONTEXT

Rivers have long been associated with human activity and land use. Providing water, food, and transportation, rivers have often been central to settlement. Ever growing populations and increasingly intensive use of land adjacent to rivers, combined with natural cycles, have brought about change in these important *natural systems*. Viewed from above, patterns of change, both recent and historical, can be observed in rivers and their *floodplains*.

THINKING CRITICALLY

On the "Athena Review" main page, scroll down to "Rivers Seen from Space."

1. Select "Nile Delta near Alexandria." Compare this photograph of the Nile delta with maps of the region in an atlas. Identify features visible in the photograph. What are some advantages of *aerial photographs* over maps? What are some disadvantages? Survey maps in the atlas to identify other rivers with similar deltas. Select "Nile Delta at Cairo." Read the caption in order to un-

derstand the use of *false color* in the image. Compare the two images. How can you use the images to evaluate land use in the Nile Delta area?

2. Select "Mississippi River at New Orleans." What is the source of this image? Make a color key to aid in the reading of this image. What does this image reveal about human settlement along the river? Speculate on the risk of flooding? Select "Mississippi Delta." In what ways is this image different from the previous one? What do these two photographs reveal about the use of color in *remotely sensed images*? Why do people choose to live near large rivers?

3. Select "The Missouri River at Glasgow, Missouri." Locate Glasgow on a large scale map in an atlas. Describe the physical landscape around Glasgow using the physical map from the atlas. Compare your map observations with the aerial photograph. What is unusual about the image? Locate areas along the river where flooding has occurred. How might federal relief agencies use aerial photographs to assess damage and assistance needs? Select "The Missouri River at Lisbon Bottom, Missouri." This site is near Glasgow. What do the colors represent in this image? Why do people use river *floodplains* for agriculture? Research the history of flooding along the Missouri River.

4. Select "The Amazon and Rio Negro at Manaus, Brazil." Locate Manaus on a map of Brazil in an atlas. Use the shuttle photograph and the atlas map to describe the physical environment of this section of the Amazon Basin. What hardships would one face in exploring this environment? Select Friar Carvajal's account of "Orellana's 1542 voyage" down the Amazon. Compare this description of a journey down the Amazon with your speculations about exploring this region.

14. THE GEO-IMAGES PROJECT: PHOTOGRAPHS OF EARTH'S LANDSCAPES

Site address: http://www-GeoImages.Berkeley.edu/GeoImages.html

Type of data: photographs

Key terms: mental image; observation; physical and human characteristics; thematic map; characteristics of place

GEOGRAPHIC CONTEXT

Geographers learn about places by observing but it is not always possible for students to visit distant places. Photographs capture places at one moment in time and create windows through which students may visit, observe, and learn. But photographs must also be used with caution since the selection of images can result in a narrow or even misleading point of view. This collection of landscape images is housed at the University of California–Berkeley.

THINKING CRITICALLY

1. California is one state for which everyone probably has *mental images* (images of place carried in one's mind). On a sheet of paper write the word "California" and immediately write down the first ten mental images that come to mind. Then on the "Geo-Image" main page scroll down and select "Images of the California Environment" and "Organized by Subject." From the list of topics, select "Agriculture" and "Urban Environment." Using the photographs, take a virtual field trip through California. Keep a journal in which you record *observations*. Select additional topics, if time permits. Now compare your journal observations with your original list of mental images. How many of your mental images were confirmed by the photographs? How many were challenged?

2. On the "Geo-Image" main page, scroll down and select "A Geographer on the Kiwai Coast of Papua New Guinea." Take a virtual trip to Papua New Guinea by examining each photograph. Record your observations in a chart that you have divided into two columns, *physical characteristics* and *human characteristics*. What clues to life in Papua New Guinea are revealed in these images? Use other sources to research Papua New Guinea further. Create a *thematic map* of this island country on which you illustrate key characteristics of place.

3. Dramatic contrasts between places can be seen in *characteristics of place* such as physical environment, people, cultural patterns, and building styles, to name but a few. Compare and contrast Hong Kong on the edge of Asia and Morocco on the edge of Africa. On the "Geo-Image" main page scroll down and select "Images of Daily Life in Morocco" and "Images of Life in Hong Kong and Environs." Examine the photographs of each place, noting in a journal similarities and differences. The differences are quickly apparent but in what ways are these two places alike? How do you account for this?

4. Assume that you have been invited to add a photograph set to the Geo-Images Project, presenting the town or region where you live. What images would you select? Why? How would your choices affect the way others view your region? Survey classmates to find out what images they would include. Are there areas of disagreement? Why? If you have access to a digital camera, create a slide show for presentation to your school.

15. VOLCANOES PAGE—PART 1

Site address: http://www.geo.mtu.edu/volcanoes/

Type of data: maps; chronological event accounts

Key terms: hazard; locational pattern; plate boundaries; human impact

GEOGRAPHIC CONTEXT

One of the most dramatic of Earth's natural forces, volcanoes can pose a serious *hazard* to human life and activity. At the same time weathered volcanic soils provide some of the most fertile agricultural lands. Volcanoes may occur along tectonic plate boundaries or at other points where magma pushes through weakened crust. Volcanoes may be explosive conic volcanoes (volcanic peak tapering to a point) or more gently erupting shield volcanoes (gently sloping, broad dome shape).

THINKING CRITICALLY

1. On the main "Volcanoes Page," select "Worldwide Volcanic Reference Map." Examine the world map and describe the *locational pattern* (where volcanoes occur) of Earth's major active volcanoes. Explain the connection between volcanoes and *plate boundaries* (edges of tectonic plates). Which volcanoes do not occur along plate boundaries? How do you account for these exceptions?

2. Below the "Worldwide Volcanic Reference Map," select under #3 "Klyuchevskoi Volcano, Kamchatka, Russia." Then select "Updates about Klyuchevskoi Volcano." Read the chronological updates from April 1993 until December 1994. Create an illustrated timeline that traces the events in this period of activity in the volcano.

3. Below the "Worldwide Volcanic Reference Map," select under #1 "Fogo Caldera, SW Cape Verde Is. Atlantic Ocean." Print copies of the maps included in the Smithsonian Bulletin reports. Then read the chronological updates on volcanic activity at Fogo and annotate the maps to show changes in the volcano and the *impacts on people* in the area. Where do people live? In what ways has the volcano disrupted their lives?

4. Below the "Worldwide Volcanic Reference Map," select under #7 "Arenal Volcano, Costa Rica." Then select "Photo Collection." Take a virtual tour of the Arenal Volcano area and record your observations in a field journal. Be sure to include observations not only of the volcano, but also of physical and human characteristics of the area around the volcano. Why do people choose to live so near to danger?

Additional sites for information on volcanoes:

Volcanoes by Robert I. Tilling (U.S. Geological Survey) (15a)

http://pubs.usgs.gov/gip/volc/

Volcano World (15b)

http://volcano.und.nodak.edu/vw.html

16. VOLCANOES PAGE—PART 2

Site address: http://www.geo.mtu.edu/volcanoes/

Type of data: maps; photographs; government reports; first person account

Key terms: sketch map; human-environment interaction; risk assessment

GEOGRAPHIC CONTEXT

Volcanoes can be very disruptive to human life. While most people will never have first-hand experience with an active volcano, those living in the shadow of a currently active volcano face many challenges, some dangerous, others merely inconvenient. Michigan Technological University provides links to most active volcanoes worldwide.

THINKING CRITICALLY

1. Under "Recent and Ongoing Volcanic Activity," select "Soufriere Hills, Montserrat, West Indies." Scroll down to "Maps" and select each of the maps available on the site. Prepare a *sketch map* on which you incorporate important physical and human characteristics of Montserrat that contribute to the complex *human-environment interaction* on this small Caribbean island. Look at the "six images" by Kevin West posted on the site. Write a descriptive caption for the sketch map you have drawn.

2. Under "Images," on the "Soufriere Hills, Montserrat, West Indies" page, select "Pictorial Archive of Activity at Soufriere Hills Volcano." Put yourself in the role of a reporter flown into Montserrat by your local newspaper to write a special feature article about the eruption of Soufriere Hills Volcano. Examine each photograph and make notes of your observations. Then write an article for the newspaper.

3. On the "Soufriere Hills, Montserrat, West Indies" page, select "Government of Montserrat and Montserrat Volcano Observatory." Scroll down to the map of "Definition of Boundary Limits and Volcanic Risk." Print a copy of the map. Then scroll to the Montserrat Volcano Observatory listing and select "Preliminary Assessment of Volcanic Risk on Montserrat, January 1998." Scan the government's *risk assessment* report, referring to the map in order to understand specific references to places on the island. Pay particular attention to the sections that address the "concept of risk" and sections that discuss risks to human welfare. Select one of the town's on Montserrat and assume you are the mayor. Prepare and present to the class a speech to the citizens of your town in which you explain the dangers and give advice on what needs to be done to ensure public safety.

4. On the "Soufriere Hills, Montserrat, West Indies" page, scroll down to "Images," and select "Chopper Flight!" Read Chris Mason's first hand account of his flight over Soufriere Hills Volcano. Evaluate his account for objectivity. What questions are raised by statements he makes? Develop a research plan to verify his account?

17. HAWAII CENTER FOR VOLCANOLOGY

Site address: http://www.soest.hawaii.edu/GG/hcv.html
Type of data: charts; maps; photographs
Key concepts: shield volcano; hotspot; crater; lava flow

GEOGRAPHIC CONTEXT

Because *shield volcanoes* (gently sloping, broad dome shape) are generally less explosive than *conic volcanoes* (volcanic peak tapering to a point), they can be studied more extensively and approached with greater safety, even when they are active. The volcanoes of Hawaii are of the shield variety and are the result of the Pacific Ocean plate's passing over the Hawaiian *hotspot*, which is currently under the island of Hawaii (the Big Island). As a result of these volcanoes, Hawaii is the only U.S. state that continues to "grow" in area. The Hawaii Center for Volcanology (HCV) is located at the University of Hawaii.

THINKING CRITICALLY

1. On the "HCV" main page, select "Hawaiian Volcanoes: Geography and Formation." Scroll down and select "Formation of the Hawaiian Islands." Examine the tables and charts to develop an explanation of how the Hawaiian Islands formed. Identify the currently active volcanoes and create a chart that illustrates how they are connected to the Hawaiian hotspot.

2. On the "HCV" main page, select "Kilauea." Kilauea is currently one of the most active volcanoes on Earth. Select "Historical Eruptions." Scroll down to the chart of historical eruptions. Create graphs that illustrate the volcano's history, including date and duration of eruptions and volume of lava produced.

3. On the "HCV" main page, select "Kilauea." The current eruption phase of Kilauea is known as Pu'u O'o and has been active since 1983. Now select "Summary of Eruption Episodes" and then "Hawaiian Volcano Observatory." Under "Kilauea," select "Eruption Update." Read the most recent update on the volcano's activity, then access the "Update archive" and read about activity at the volcano over the past several years. Design a National Park Service brochure for tourists visiting the volcano. Point out important features to see, as well as advice for personal safety. Include a map with symbols keyed to the points of interest.

4. On the "HCV" main page, select "Kilauea." Scroll to the bottom of the page and select " 'virtual' field trips." Select the "Tour around Kilauea Crater." Proceed with the tour, making observations in a field journal. What are the characteristics of a shield volcano? What does the *crater* look like? What evidence of past activity can you observe? Continue your tour by selecting the "Tour along Chain of Craters Road." How have *lava flows* altered the landscape of the island? Complete your tour by selecting "What's New at the Volcano." This regularly updated feature is also archived so that you can trace recent events at the volcano. What is currently happening at Kilauea? Review your "field notes" and write a summary of what you have seen and learned while visiting Kilauea Volcano.

18. THE WORLD-WIDE EARTHQUAKE LOCATOR

Site address: http://www.geo.ed.ac.uk/quakes/quakes.html

Type of data: statistical data sets; maps

Key terms: earthquakes; seismic; seismologist; magnitude

GEOGRAPHIC CONTEXT

Earthquakes are one of Earth's most destructive natural events. Major earthquakes receive much public and media attention, but minor earthquakes occur with much greater frequency. Knowing where and why earthquakes occur helps people make informed choices about where they want to live. In addition, by keeping careful records of these *seismic* (relating to an earthquake) events, scientists (called *seismologists*) hope to be able some day to predict when and where major earthquakes will occur. Records of earthquakes occurring around the world are kept on this archival site.

THINKING CRITICALLY

1. On the main page of the site, scroll down and select "World-Wide Earthquake Locator." Print the list of most recent earthquakes. Sort the earthquakes by *magnitude* (measure of total energy released). Then, on a blank world map, locate each earthquake using symbols to distinguish different levels of magnitude. What patterns can you observe? How do you account for areas of greater frequency?

2. On the main page of the site, scroll down and select "World-Wide Earthquake Locator." Scroll to the bottom of this page and select the "World Map" icon. Earthquakes worldwide are indicated on the map. Describe the pattern of occurrence. What areas seem to be most prone to earthquakes? What areas are least prone to earthquakes? How do you account for this pattern? Select the area near Japan to view a larger scale map. What pattern can be observed? How do you account for the arc shape of the pattern?

3. On the main page of the site, scroll down and select "World-Wide Earthquake Locator." Scroll to the bottom of the page and select the "U.S. Map" icon. Where in the United States are earthquakes most likely to occur? Select the area of California in order to view a larger scale map. Describe the pattern of earthquake occurrence. Compare this map with a political map of California showing major cities and highways. What would be the consequence of a major earthquake in this area?

4. On the main page of the site, scroll down and select "World-Wide Earthquake Locator." From the list of recent earthquakes, select one major event (magnitude 5.0 or above) to view a larger scale map of the area. Research the country or region affected. Develop a profile of the likely human impact of this earth-

quake. Then search for newspaper articles that report on the impact of the earthquake. For example, *The Washington Post* site (18a) (http://www.washingtonpost.com) provides access to its archives as well as links to other news outlets around the world.

Additional sites for information on earthquakes:

National Earthquake Information Center (18b)

http://earthquake.usgs.gov

Earthquakes by Kaye M. Shedlock and Louis C. Pakiser (U.S. Geological Survey) (18c)

http://pubs.usgs.gov/gip/earthq1/index.html

Surfing the Internet for Earthquake Data (18d)

http://www.geophys.washington.edu/seismosurfing.html

19. WORLDCLIMATE

Site address: http://www.worldclimate.com/

Type of data: climate data sets

Key terms: climate; climate zones; temperature; precipitation; vegetation; latitude; elevation

GEOGRAPHIC CONTEXT

Climate (long-term average weather) is one of the major distinguishing physical characteristics of place. Using various defining criteria, climatologists have divided Earth's surface into major *climate zones* based on shared characteristics of *temperature* and *precipitation*. Other climatologists have defined climate zones in terms of predominant *vegetation* types. Regardless of the defining criteria chosen, climate patterns are largely the result of a combination of factors including latitude, landforms, location relative to water, prevailing winds, and ocean currents. "WorldClimate.com" is a large database of long-term climate averages for more than 85,000 locations. Simple online instructions direct users in the retrieval of data.

THINKING CRITICALLY

1. *Latitude* plays a major role in determining the climate of a given location. Test this statement by gathering average temperature and precipitation data for several locations along a common line of longitude but at different latitudes. For example, collect data for Kinshasa (4°S), Tripoli (32°N), Budapest (47°N),

and Uppsala (59°N). Construct and compare climate graphs for each location. Explain the relationship between latitude and climate.

2. Investigate the role of determining factors other than latitude by collecting data for the following locations, all of which are at approximately the same latitude: San Francisco, CA (122°W), Colorado Springs, CO (104°W), Wichita, KS (97°W), Lexington, KY (84°W), and Richmond, VA (77°W). Construct a set of climate graphs. Analyze the graphs as well as a physical map of the United States. How do you account for the differences in the graphs? What other factors influence the climate of a given location? How can you test your conclusions?

3. Investigate the effect of *elevation* on the climate of a particular location. Collect data for the following locations in Ecuador: Guayaquil (elev. 13 feet) and Quito (elev. 9226 feet). Construct climate graphs for each location. Analyze the graphs and form a generalization about the effects of elevation on climate. Test your generalization by evaluating data for other locations at similar latitudes, but different elevations.

4. Collect climate data for several locations within your state. Construct and analyze climate graphs for each. Do the graphs vary significantly? Why? Why not? Examine a *vegetation* map for your state. How is vegetation related to climate?

20. WEATHER UNDERGROUND

Site address: http://www.wunderground.com

Type of data: near real-time statistical data sets

Key terms: climate; weather

GEOGRAPHIC CONTEXT

Unlike *climate*, which represents a long-term average, *weather* is the day-to-day condition of the atmosphere at a given place and time. Weather is what we observe around us, whether cold and windy or hot and humid. Current weather data allows observation of daily variations that are often lost in the averages of climate statistics. Weather data allows comparison of places in different climate zones, as well as within a single zone. The "Weather Underground" provides access to the most current weather information, as well as some historical data for most locations in the United States.

THINKING CRITICALLY

1. Using an atlas, locate a climate map of the United States. What are the characteristics (temperature and precipitation) that define each climate region in the country? *Climate* is a long-term average. Compare the climate map with

the current weather map of the United States on the "Weather Underground" main page. How much variation is there between climate averages and daily *weather* conditions? How might this affect decision-making if you were planning a trip?

2. Use the "Fast Forecast" search box to determine current weather conditions in Washington, D.C. Record data for temperature, humidity, and barometric pressure. Use the drop-down menu to determine weather conditions at other recording stations in the Washington, D.C. metropolitan area. Is there variation? Why? Why not? Use other maps of the Washington, D.C. area to speculate on local conditions that might account for variations in weather conditions within the metropolitan area. Track the data for Washington, D.C. and surrounding stations for several days to determine if these variations are a coincidence or part of a pattern. Present your findings in a set of graphs.

3. Use the "Fast Forecast" search box to determine current weather conditions in Atlanta, GA. Record the data for temperature (maximum and minimum), humidity, and barometric pressure. Use the "Historical Conditions" drop-down menu to collect the same data for past years for Atlanta? Graph the data you have collected. Is there much variation? Repeat this process for a different time of year. What are your findings?

4. Use the "Fast Forecast" search box to determine current weather conditions in your city or town. Collect data for several days. Compare the data collected with weather maps in a local newspaper. Then write a weather bulletin describing conditions in the local area.

5. Using the current weather map of the United States, select your state. Use data in the chart of weather stations in the state to create maps of weather conditions. Do conditions vary greatly within your state? Why? Why not? What patterns in the physical geography of the state influence local weather conditions? Create a bulletin board display that explains weather patterns in your state.

21. NATIONAL HURRICANE CENTER

Site address: http://www.nhc.noaa.gov/

Type of data: data sets; maps

Key terms: low pressure system; hurricane; meteorologist; storm track

GEOGRAPHIC CONTEXT

Tropical *low pressure systems* known as *hurricanes* are the largest storm systems on Earth. Packing winds above 75 miles per hour for even the lowest category storm, hurricanes bring destruction and sometimes death to the southeastern region of the United States each year. In addition to strong winds associated with hurricanes, heavy rains and unusually high tides, known as storm surges, flood low-lying areas. These low pressure storms are not unique to the United States. They also occur in the Indian Ocean where they are called cyclones, in the western Pacific Ocean where they are called typhoons, and in the eastern Pacific Ocean where they are called hurricanes. The "National Hurricane Center" (NHC) maintains extensive records on tropical storm activity.

THINKING CRITICALLY

Scroll to the bottom of the "NHC" main page. Select and print copies of the Atlantic hurricane tracking chart.

1. On the "NHC" main page, under "Current Season," select "Active Cyclones and Advisories." Depending on the time of the year (hurricane season is from June through October), record recent storm activity. Plot each storm on a tracking map. What are predictions for storm activity for the current season? Research how *meteorologists* develop their storm predictions.

2. On the "NHC" main page, under "Historical Data," select "Past Seasons." Then select the text report for Atlantic hurricanes in 1998. How many hurricanes were there in 1998? Scroll down to "1998 Color Track Map" and select this image. Study this map of *storm tracks*. What generalizations can you make about Atlantic hurricane tracks? How can you test this generalization?

3. On the "NHC" main page, under "Historical Data," select "Past Seasons." Then select the text report for Atlantic hurricanes in 1998. From the list of storms in 1998, select "Hurricane Georges." Scroll through the document to Table 1. "Preliminary Best Track." Use a "Hurricane Tracking Chart" to plot the storm's progress. Use different colors to note the changing stages of the storm. How can you indicate time on the chart? Label points of "landfall" along the storm's path. Construct a graph to show changes in barometric pressure and wind speed as the storm progressed. Scroll to Table 5. "Death and Insured Damage Estimates." Create graphs that summarize the human toll of the storm. Write a newspaper article that summarizes the effects of Hurricane Georges. Use maps and graphs to highlight key points.

4. On the "NHC" main page, under "Historical Data," select "Past Seasons." Then scroll down and select "U.S. Strikes by State." Create a choropleth map that shows the total number of storms to strike each state, Texas to Maine, from 1900 to 1996. Create a second map that shows the incidence of "major" storms. Create a graph that shows the occurrence of major hurricanes by month for the same region. Write a report in which you speculate on the probability of serious storm damage at different places and times along the U.S. Atlantic coast.

22. TORNADO PROJECT ONLINE

Site address: http://www.tornadoproject.com
Type of data: data sets; personal accounts
Key terms: tornado; Fujita Scale; storm chasers

GEOGRAPHIC CONTEXT

While not as large in areal extent as hurricanes, *tornadoes* are the most powerful and destructive storms on Earth. They form as low pressure systems over land, and while they may occur in any mid-latitude continental area, they occur with greatest frequency in the interior plains region of the United States, often referred to as "tornado alley." "The Tornado Project Online" is an archive of storm data, personal accounts, and historical records about tornado activity in the United States.

THINKING CRITICALLY

1. On the "Tornado Project" main page, select "Tornado Stories." Read these accounts of actual tornadoes. Develop a profile of characteristics of these dangerous storms. For example, what is the storm like? What types of property damage occur? What is the human cost? Form a set of generalizations about tornadoes. Then extend your research to test your generalizations.

2. On the "Tornado Project" main page, select "Tornado Top Tens." On a blank map of the United States, locate and label by place and date the ten worst tornadoes to strike this country. Make a bar graph showing the human toll of these storms. What patterns can be observed in the map? What do you notice about the dates on which these storms occurred? Is there a season when tornadoes are more likely to strike? Were these storms more dangerous in the past than today? Explain your conclusions?

3. On the "Tornado Project" main page, select "All Tornadoes." Scroll down to the map of the United States and select your state. Create a poster on which you have a map of the state. Locate each storm occurrence, using color-coded symbols to indicated storm intensity (*Fujita Scale*). Add a graph on which you compare deaths and injuries each year. Compare your state to a state in "Tornado Alley."

4. On the "Tornado Project" main page, select "Storm Chasing." Tours are available for people interested in observing a tornado first hand. Several journals of *storm chasers* are available on this page. Select several and read these first hand descriptions. What observations do these accounts have in common? What did these people learn to look for as they searched for tornado conditions? How accurate do you think these accounts are? How can you evaluate first hand accounts for accuracy?

23. NATURAL HAZARDS

Site address: http://www.usgs.gov/themes/hazard.html

Type of data: maps; statistical data sets; narrative

Key terms: natural events; hazards; landslide; earthquake; wildfire

GEOGRAPHIC CONTEXT

Natural events, such as floods, storms, or earthquakes, become *hazards* when they put human populations and property at risk. As the population of the United States increases, more and more people are moving into areas affected by hazardous natural events. The U.S. Geological Survey (USGS) monitors hazards throughout the country and issues information related to public safety.

THINKING CRITICALLY

1. On the "USGS Hazards" main page, select "Geographic Distribution of Hazards." Access the map for "Groundshaking Hazards." Which areas are most vulnerable to earthquakes? Compare this map with a population distribution map in an atlas. What major population centers are at risk of earthquakes? Repeat this process with the remaining five hazard maps. Then view the combined map at the bottom of the page. In the areas not affected by any of these hazards, what is the population density? Why do people choose to live in areas affected by hazards?

2. On the "USGS Hazards" main page, select "Individual Hazards." Then select "Landslides" and "National Landslide Information Center." Access and read the article "Liquid Earth." Why did the author choose this title for her article? As you read, collect information about the location, causes, and consequences of *landslides*. Use what you have learned to look with new eyes at the area where you live. Are there places that could be subject to landslides? Develop an action plan to protect human life and property.

3. On the "USGS Hazards" main page, select "Earthquakes." Then select "Southern California Earthquake Information," "Future," "More Hazard and Preparedness Information," and "Earthquake Preparedness." No one can prevent another *earthquake* in California but people can take steps to ensure their safety. Select "Next Big Earthquake in the Bay Area." Scan the various advisories; then prepare a clear, illustrated brochure advising people what to do to protect themselves. Decide which information is most important and how you can present it so that people will take it seriously.

4. On the "USGS Hazards" main page, select "Wildfires." Then select "National Interagency Fire Center," "Current Wildland Fire Information," and "1998 Fire Season at a Glance." Under "Statistics," select "10 Largest Fires of 1998" and "Historical Comparisons." How many of the largest fires of 1998 were near populated areas? How did the fires of 1998 compare to past years? What factors might affect the number of fires in a given year? Return to "1998 Fire Season at a Glance" and select "U.S. Highlights." Read about the Florida wildland fires? Why did these fires occur? Do any of these conditions exist in the area where you live? Is your region vulnerable to *wildfires*? What actions could be taken to prevent wildfires?

24. DROUGHT

Site address: http://enso.unl.edu/ndmc/index.html

Type of data: maps; charts; statistical data sets

Key terms: drought; forecast; precipitation variability; Dust Bowl

GEOGRAPHIC CONTEXT

Drought occurs when precipitation falls below expected amounts for an extended period of time. It is a normal meteorological phenomenon that affects all parts of the United States, as well as the rest of the world, from time to time. Farmers feel the effects of drought as crops wither and die but other people also are affected by water shortages and rising prices of goods that are dependent on a regular supply of water. The National Drought Mitigation Center (NDMC) monitors drought conditions and advises on risk management.

THINKING CRITICALLY

1. On the "NDMC" main page, select "Drought Science." Read the different definitions of "drought." Then read "Prospects for Predicting Drought." Create an illustrated public information brochure that explains in simple terms what drought is and what we can do about it.

2. On the "NDMC" main page, select "Drought Watch." Select "Current Droughts Affecting the United States" and use the interactive map to read detailed reports about those states most affected. What are some consequences of drought in these states? What is the long-term *forecast*? Use links within each report to access graphs showing precipitation patterns. Assume the role of a television reporter and prepare a "special report" for the evening newscast, detailing current drought conditions. Include maps and graphs that convey the main points visually.

3. On the "NDMC" main page, select "Climatology." Scroll down to "Drought Climatology" and select "Map out past droughts." Using the map search function, plot a series of maps for the United States at, for example, ten-year intervals. Note the patterns of *precipitation variability* over time. Do some areas seem to be more drought prone that others? What about your state? Are droughts a common occurrence there? Return to the "Drought Climatology" menu and scroll down to "Historical maps . . ." and "Historical graphs. . . ." Examine these time series maps and graphs. Write an essay in which you address the topic, "Drought in the United States—A Common or Uncommon Event?"

4. One of the best known droughts in U.S. history was the famous "Dust Bowl" event of the 1930s. Research this event by selecting "Impacts" from the "NDMC" main page. Scroll down to "Impacts and Mitigation of Drought in

the Dust Bowl Years." Read different accounts of this devastating drought. Then script a role-play in which different speakers tell about their experiences during the Dust Bowl.

Additional Dust Bowl sites:

Multiple links to Dust Bowl sites, supported by Connecticut State University (24a)

http://www.ecsu.ctstateu.edu/depts/edu/textbooks/dustbowl.html

Excerpts from *Dust Bowl Diary* (1934) (24b)

http://chnm.gmu.edu/courses/hist409/dust/low.html

25. NOAA PHOTO COLLECTION: IMAGES OF THE NATURAL WORLD

Site address: http://www.photolib.noaa.gov/

Type of data: photographs

Key terms: tropical islands; tornadoes; coral reef; human intervention

GEOGRAPHIC CONTEXT

Photographs take us to places and events in the natural world that may otherwise be inaccessible. Nevertheless, seeing weather phenomena, remote land and water features, and wildlife enables viewers to put places in clearer perspective. The National Oceanic and Atmospheric Administration (NOAA) photo archives invite study and analysis of the physical environment.

THINKING CRITICALLY

1. On the "NOAA Photo Collection" main page, select "Islands in the Sun." Select one of the regional options, for example, "Equatorial Pacific." Examine the extensive collection of photographs noting characteristics, both natural and human, of these islands. Select 8–10 images and copy them to a file on your computer. Be sure to note the location shown in each image as well as the source. Use the images and presentation software, for example, Microsoft PowerPoint, to create an electronic travel brochure, inviting others to visit these *tropical islands*.

2. On the "NOAA Photo Collection" main page, select "Photo Albums." Select the "National Severe Storms Laboratory Collection" and "Tornadoes." Examine the photographs of these severe storms. What common characteristics can you observe about *tornadoes*? Research tornadoes (see [22] http://www.tornadoproject.com) to develop a profile for where and when these

storms are most likely to occur. Prepare a public safety announcement that reminds people of what they should do in the event of a tornado in the area.

3. On the "NOAA Photo Collection" main page select "Photo Albums." Select the "Coral Kingdom." Examine the photographs of vertebrates and invertebrates common to the *coral reefs* of the Pacific Ocean and Caribbean and Red Seas. What types of living things inhabit coral reefs? Do you observe differences among the reefs of these three regions? Under what conditions do coral reefs develop? How has human intervention placed these formations at risk? Prepare and defend an advocacy paper that argues for the protection of coral reefs.

4. On the "NOAA Photo Collection" main page, select "Photo Albums." Select the "Paths Less Taken" and "The Antarctic." Antarctica is one of the most forbidding environments on Earth. Examine the photographs in "The Traverses" and "90 South." What special preparation is required of explorers and scientists who work in the Antarctic? Research the scientific stations in Antarctica. What countries are involved? How many people live in these stations? What provisions have been made to protect this fragile environment? Examine other photographs in the collection. What changes has *human intervention* already brought to Antarctica?

26. FEMA VIRTUAL LIBRARY & ELECTRONIC READING ROOM: IMAGES OF THE NATURAL WORLD

Site address: http://www.fema.gov/library/photo.htm

Type of data: photographs

Key terms: natural hazard; FEMA; federal assistance; tornado; flood; hurricane; fire

GEOGRAPHIC CONTEXT

Natural hazards are extreme events of nature that inflict damage, injury, and even death on human populations living in their path. Included among such hazards are hurricanes, tornadoes, earthquakes, floods, and fires. Much can be learned about these hazards and their effects on human uses of Earth by studying photographs from the archives of the Federal Emergency Management Agency (FEMA).

THINKING CRITICALLY

Open the "FEMA Photo Library" main page.

1. Scroll down to the "1998 Alabama Tornado." Examine the photographs of storm damage following this *tornado*. Put yourself in the role of a FEMA field investigator. Write up your report on this storm and make recommendations

for *federal assistance*. What are the long-term needs of these communities? What are the immediate and short-term needs? Why does the area affected by this storm require external assistance?

2. Scroll down to the "1998 California Floods." On a large scale map of California, locate and label the communities included in this collection of photographs. Speculate on the connection between location and *flood* vulnerability. Examine the photographic record of this flood. What types of damage occurred? Classify the types of damage. For example, categories might include physical landscape, infrastructure, personal property. Why do people choose to live in areas prone to hazards? Should there be regulations limiting construction in such areas? Conduct a debate on this issue.

3. Scroll down to "Hurricane Marilyn." What place was affected by this destructive storm? Why was FEMA involved? Survey the photographs of storm damage. Based on your observations of storm damage, write a script for a live-on-the-scene television report during the *hurricane*. What would you see? What would you hear? Continue your report on the morning after the storm has passed. What appeals for assistance would you report? What special needs are associated with being on an island?

4. Scroll down to the "1998 Florida Fires." Examine the photographs of the Florida *fires*. What measures were taken to protect personal property? Aside from personal property loss, what other problems resulted from these fires? Can such fires be avoided? Prepare a public awareness brochure outlining steps that people can take to prevent fires and to protect themselves and their property when fires do occur.

27. FOREST FRONTIERS INITIATIVE

Site address: http://www.wri.org/wri/ffi/

Type of data: maps; data sets

Key terms: resource; frontier forest; choropleth map

GEOGRAPHIC CONTEXT

About a third of Earth's land area is under forest cover. Forests are a critical *resource*: rich in biodiversity, a source of plant and animal products with both commercial and aesthetic value, and an important link in the carbon-oxygen exchange cycle. Many of Earth's great forests are threatened due to such activities as logging, mining, ranching, and other development schemes. Some scientists fear that loss of forests may contribute to global warming trends, thus putting other ecosystems at risk as well. World Resources Institute, a non-governmental organization, monitors and collects data on environmental conditions worldwide.

THINKING CRITICALLY

1. The World Resources Institute defines a *frontier forest* as an area of natural forest that remains "ecologically intact." On the "FFI" main page, scroll down and select "Interactive Forest Maps." Examine the map carefully and write a narrative description of the distribution of frontier forests 8,000 years ago. Then describe the distribution of current frontier forests. Which areas have experienced the greatest loss of frontier forests? Summarize your observations on a poster chart on which you show areas of major loss. Include a column in which you speculate on human actions that account for these losses.

2. On the "FFI" main page, select "Climate, Biodiversity, and Forests." Then select "Biodiversity and Climate" and "The Last Frontier Forests" (note: the direct link is [27a] http://www.wri.org/wri/ffi/lff-eng/). From the side bar select "Table: Total Area in Original, Current and Frontier Forest." Examine the data presented in the table and select appropriate types of graphs for presenting the data in a visual manner that conveys the message of forest loss. Make a map to complement the graphs, showing areas of greatest loss.

3. On the "FFI" main page, select "Climate, Biodiversity, and Forests." Then select "Biodiversity and Climate" and "The Last Frontier Forests" (note: the direct link is [27a] http://www.wri.org/wri/ffi/lff-eng/). Select "Frontier Forest Index." Use the "Frontier Forest Index" in the last column of the table to construct a *choropleth map* of countries with frontier forests. Use the categories provided in the table to organize classes of data on the map. Examine the map and identify patterns in terms of degree of loss. Do countries of greatest loss share any common characteristics?

4. On the "FFI" main page, select "Climate, Biodiversity, and Forests." Then select "Biodiversity and Climate" and "The Last Frontier Forests" (note: the direct link is [27a] http://www.wri.org/wri/ffi/lff-eng/). Select "Threats to Frontier Forests." Examine this table of major threats to forests. Plan a debate in which competing interests consider the future of frontier forests in Central America (or any other region of special interest). Interest groups might include environmentalists, loggers, miners, and commercial and subsistence farmers.

28. EVERGLADES PHOTO TOUR

Site address: http://www.eng.fiu.edu/evrglads/enp_phot/topdoc.htm

Type of data: photographs

Key terms: wetland; plant life; habitat; human intervention

GEOGRAPHIC CONTEXT

The Everglades National Park is one of North America's natural treasures. A vast *wetland* area covering much of south Florida, this "sea of grass" is habitat to unique creatures. It is also the source of much of the region's fresh water. Under pressure from competing interests of urban dwellers, commercial farmers, and environmentalists, this wetland is at risk. Florida International University maintains an extensive resource collection related to the Everglades.

THINKING CRITICALLY

Open the "Everglades Photo Tour" main page.

1. Select "Everglades Plant Life." Progress through the slides, making notes about the types and diversity of *plant life* in the Everglades. Create a poster on which you illustrate and identify types of vegetation typical of this wetland ecosystem. Research other wetlands and compare vegetation found there with that of the Everglades. How do you account for the similarities and differences?

2. Select "Wildlife!!" Make a list of the wildlife shown in the slides. Classify the list according to land animals, water animals, birds, and insects. In what special ways does the Everglades ecosystem provide a critical *habitat* for these living creatures? Are any of these creatures on the endangered species list? How might human interventions have put these creatures at risk?

3. Select "Structures at ENP." The slides in this set reveal some of the *human interventions* in the Everglades ecosystem. In what specific ways have people altered the ecosystem? Why have people intervened in the Everglades? Create a chart with two headings: positive; negative. Sort the human interventions by these categories and explain each. Can some interventions be both positive and negative?

4. Scroll to the bottom of the page and select "Save ENP!" Over the past 150 years, more than two-thirds of Florida's wetlands have been altered by people. In recent years, however, various government agencies at all levels have attempted to reverse the direction of change. Observe the "Online Environmental Simulator" to identify some of the issues facing the Everglades. Then select the "Interview with Marianno Guardo" to learn more. Consider the issues and arguments presented. Decide where you stand. Then write a position paper in which you present well-reasoned arguments for what should be done about the Everglades.

"People are central to geography in that human activities help shape Earth's surface, human settlements and structures are part of Earth's surface, and humans compete for control of Earth's surface" (*Geography for Life* 1994: 35). Human systems are a cornerstone of geographic understanding because:

- the dynamic characteristics of human populations—fertility, mortality, mobility—vary widely on Earth and make each place unique.
- human populations are rarely static; people are constantly moving in response to counterbalancing factors that propel and attract them. And as they move they change and shape the landscapes around them.
- different groups of people perceive and respond to opportunities and limitations through the lens of their unique cultures. The result is a mosaic of humanity giving character and uniqueness to different places.
- different groups, each with its own sense of place, have divided Earth's surface according to their perception of territory. When these emotional boundaries, defined by culture and shared history, overlap, conflict may result.

29. STATISTICAL ABSTRACT OF THE UNITED STATES

Site address: http://www.census.gov/statab/www/index.html

Type of data: statistical data

Key terms: population profile; sex ratio; age structure; regional distribution; aggregate; choropleth map

GEOGRAPHIC CONTEXT

The *Statistical Abstract of the United States* makes available in quantitative format data on demographic, social, and economic characteristics of the country. Such data provide the basis for comparison and analysis at multiple scales, including state, county, and metropolitan area. Governments, businesses, schools, and public services rely upon statistical profiles in order to make informed decisions. The ability to read and use statistics is a fundamental skill for all geographers.

THINKING CRITICALLY

Open the "Statistical Abstract" main page.

1. Select "USA Statistics in Brief" to locate national summary data. Select "Population." Create graphs that *profile* the U.S. population since the 1990 census. Include in the profile graphs that examine such characteristics as *sex ratio* (males per 100 females in the population), *age structure* (proportion of males and females in each age category), racial and ethnic structure, and regional distribution. Examine the graphs and write an essay that describes trends and patterns in population dynamics in the United States. Prepare a set of research questions that are raised by your graphs.

2. Select "USA Statistics in Brief" to locate national summary data. Select "Population." Scroll down to the *regional distribution* (%) of population. What percent of total population lived in each major census region in 1998? These percents are based on *aggregate* numbers and disguise uneven distribution among the states of each region. Return to "USA Statistics in Brief" and select "State population estimates." Create maps of the United States showing the ten states with the largest populations and the ten states with the highest percent increase in population since 1990. What patterns are revealed? Based on recent trends, speculate on the results of the next census.

3. Select "State Rankings." Select "Population Under 18 Years Old" and "Population 65 Years Old and Over." Divide the states into five groups according to the percent of the population under 18 and the percent of population 65 and over. Then create *choropleth maps* (maps using graded color values to represent relative data values) to show the age structure of the country by state. Which states vary significantly from the national averages of 25.9 percent under 18 years and 12.7 percent 65 years and over? What factors might account for these variations?

4. Select "State profiles." On the interactive map, select your state and then select "State profile." Collect data about population, income and poverty, and economic activity in your state and create a set of maps and graphs that profile the state. Return to the interactive state map and select your county. Create another profile, this time for your county. Then compare your county with the state. What do you observe? Use your knowledge of the local area to account for any differences.

30. SELECTED HISTORICAL CENSUS DATA: POPULATION: 1790 TO 1990

Site address: http://www.census.gov/population/www/censusdata/pop-hc. html

Select: "Population and Housing Counts—Table 2. Population: 1790 to 1990" (Note: This PDF document requires *Adobe Acrobat Reader* which is available for download at no cost.)

Type of data: statistical data set

Key terms: population growth; natural increase; migration; census region

GEOGRAPHIC CONTEXT

In order to understand any country, its population must be understood. The first census of the United States was conducted in 1790. This enumeration of the population is mandated by the Constitution and occurs every ten years. The *population's growth* is the net result of *natural increase* (births minus deaths) and *migration*. Patterns of population growth reflect social and economic conditions, as well as the political climate both within the country and in the world beyond. As the population has grown, people have altered the physical and cultural landscapes. Such changes are central to the study of geography. The U.S. Bureau of the Census conducts a census of the U.S. population every ten years.

THINKING CRITICALLY

Open the PDF document "Population: 1790 to 1990."

1. Using data from the beginning of the table, create a graph that shows the changing U.S. population from 1790 to 1990. When were periods of greatest growth? What historical events can you associate with periods of high growth? The Census Bureau divides the country into four *regions*: Northeast, Midwest, South, and West. Create a series of graphs that show the growth of population in each region from 1790 to 1990. How are these graphs different from the national graphs? What do they reveal about the country's growth?

2. The table also provides statistics for each individual state. Which state had the largest population at the time of the 1790 census? Which state had the largest population in 1890? Which state had the largest population in 1990? Create a set of graphs that show the changing population of these three states from 1790 to 1990. Use these graphs as the basis for a discussion of changing demographic patterns in the United States. How does the demographic history of these three states parallel the country's history?

3. Locate your state in the table. Create a graph that shows the growth of population in your state from 1790 (or from the first census in which your state was counted) to 1990. Compare your state's demographic history with that of the country. Is your state experiencing population change at a rate higher or lower than the national average? How do you account for this?

4. Return to the "Selected Historical Census Data" page of the U.S. Census Bureau. Under "The Population of States and Counties of the United States: 1790 to 1990," scroll down to select the "extract of the historical census data." This file contains county-level data for each state from 1900 to 1990. Select your state. Calculate the rate of population increase by decade for the United States, for your state, and for the county in which you live. Compare the rates of increase. How do you account for any differences? Scan the data for your state. Are there counties that have experienced either unusually rapid growth

or negative growth? Form a hypothesis about why these counties have experienced such growth. Then undertake research to test your hypothesis.

31. GOVERNMENT INFORMATION SHARING PROJECT: USA COUNTIES 1996

Site address: http://govinfo.kerr.orst.edu/usaco-stateis.html

Type of data: census data sets; maps

Key terms: diversity; aggregate; race; elderly

GEOGRAPHIC CONTEXT

While the United States is one country, it is characterized by tremendous internal *diversity*. Statistics analyzed at the national or even state level mask much of this diversity because numbers are *aggregated*, or collected as a whole, and thus variation is lost. County level data provides a more accurate picture of demographic, economic, and political characteristics and variations, and consequently allow more detailed comparison and analysis both within and between states. Oregon State University Information Services provides a direct link to "USA Counties 1996" within the massive data files of the U.S. Census Bureau and tools for making comparisons and profiles.

THINKING CRITICALLY

Access the interactive map of the United States on the Oregon State University "Government Information Sharing Project" main page.

1. On the interactive map of the United States, select the state of "Texas." On the "Texas" page, select "State of Texas," and then "Summary Report." The summary report includes *aggregated* data for the entire state. Use the data in this table to create a graphic profile of the state's population. Return to the interactive U.S. map and select "New York." Create a graphic profile of New York. Compare these two states. What similarities and differences do you observe? Why do you think these similarities or differences exist?

2. On the interactive map of the United States, select the state of "California." On the "California" page, select "State of California." Use the drop down menu under "Summary Report" to examine the data choices available. Which table will allow you to analyze the *racial* composition of California's population? ("Population, Total and Selected Characteristics") What racial groups are identified in census data? (Note: "Hispanic" is an ethnicity, NOT a racial category.) What proportion of California's population is in each racial group? Has this proportion changed over the time period of the data included in the table? Represent this data graphically.

3. On the site main page, select "AREA COMPARISONS—GRAPHICAL OP-TIONS." Then on the interactive map of the United States, select the state of "Florida." Florida is known as a retirement state, but is this an accurate assumption? Scroll down and select "Percent Population 65 Years and Over, 1995." When the data is loaded, select the "Map Distribution" option. Examine the map of Florida showing the population 65 years and over. Is the *elderly* population evenly distributed throughout the state? Use maps and other resources to determine why the percent of elderly population is higher in some counties than others. Why is it lower, for example, in Dade County where Miami is located?

4. On the site main page, select "AREA COMPARISONS—GRAPHICAL OP-TIONS." Then on the interactive map of the United States, select your state. Look at the data options on the state page. Develop a short questionnaire about distribution patterns within your state based on the categories in the list of data variables. Administer the questionnaire in your school or community. Then create county-based maps for the same variables. Compare the survey results with the census-based maps. How well do people know their own state? Are there any misconceptions? Why do you think this is the case?

32. CHILDREN IN THE STATES: 1998 DATA

Site address: http://www.childrensdefense.org/states/data.html

Type of data: statistical data sets

Key terms: productive cohort; advocate; rate; choropleth map

GEOGRAPHIC CONTEXT

When demographic data sets present statistics for an entire population, the needs and special interests of particular groups may be overlooked in the broad picture. One such group is children. Emphasis is often on *productive cohorts*, that portion of the population between the ages of 20 and 60 when people are most likely to be working, but children also require the attention and efforts of researchers. Areas of concern include such topics as health, education, economic circumstances, and living conditions. The Children's Defense Fund is a children's advocacy group.

THINKING CRITICALLY

Access "Children in the States" main page.

1. Marian Wright Edelman is an outspoken *advocate* for the rights of children. In the sidebar of this site, select "A Voice for Children" to access a series of statements by Edelman. Read several examples from the online archive and evaluate them for objectivity, accuracy, and relevance. Develop a set of ques-

tions to guide your evaluation. What resources do you need access to in order to make a fair assessment of her position?

2. Select the "Profile" for the United States. Scroll down to the tables and use the data to create a graphic profile of the status of children in the United States. What criteria will you use? Why? Use your profile as the basis for a letter to your Congressman concerning the status of children in the United States. What position will you take? What action will you advocate? Support your argument with compelling evidence.

3. Select the "Profile" for your state. What is the status of children in your state compared to national averages? Create a set of graphs that compare important indicators for your state and the country overall. What indicators will you choose? Why? Are there areas in which your state falls below the national average? Interview someone at a local social service agency to find out what services are available in your community for children who are in need. Develop an action plan to address the needs of children in your state and community.

4. Select the "Profile" for the United States. Scan the data options in the tables for the national profile. Select a *rate* (not a number since states vary in size of total population) that you consider an important indicator of the status of children in the country, for example, "Infant mortality rate" or "Percentage of children under 18 who are poor." Note the national average; then collect the data for each state and the District of Columbia. Create a *choropleth map* (a map using graded color values to represent relative data values) showing variation in the selected indicator among the states. Analyze the patterns revealed. How do you account for states that vary, either higher or lower, from the national average? Where does your state fall?

33. CHILDREN'S RIGHTS COUNCIL

Site address: http://www.vix.com/crc/

Type of data: statistical data; narrative

Key terms: advocacy group; bias; objectivity; point of view; choropleth map; aggregate data

GEOGRAPHIC CONTEXT

Census data is an important source of information about populations or subsets of a population. However, other sources also provide data about population groups as well. *Advocacy groups* may use data from multiple sources to advance a particular point of view. Such information is useful but must be approached with care to avoid *bias*. The Children's Rights Council is an advocacy group that focuses on the special circumstances and needs of children, a subset of the population that is unable to speak out on its own behalf.

THINKING CRITICALLY

Open the "Children's Rights Council" main page and select "The Best States to Raise Children."

1. Scroll down on the page and read the "Press Release" issued with the ranking of states. Evaluate this document for *objectivity*. Print a copy of the press release and highlight those words or phrases that reflect the organization's particular *point of view*. Circle words or statistics that you feel should be verified in order to make the statement more convincing. Evaluate the criteria used to rank the states. Do you think these are the best criteria or do these criteria lead to a biased ranking? Write an editorial in which you present your point of view regarding this ranking.

2. Scroll down on the page to the table "Ranking of States." Construct a *choropleth map* (a map using graded color values to represent relative data values), using five data classes, on which you show the ranking of states. Do you observe any patterns? Do the states in a given class on the map share any particular characteristics, other than the stated criteria? Prepare a list of shared characteristics based on your own evaluation. Then conduct research to test your hypothesis? What generalizations can you make?

3. Scroll down on the page to the table of state summaries by specific criteria. Locate your state in the list. Consider the individual criteria. These are aggregate numbers or rates for the state as a whole. Does the use of *aggregate data* present an objective picture of the entire state? Research several of the criteria in the list for individual counties in your state. Does this create a different picture of the state? Create your own report on the "Best Counties in My State to Raise Children."

4. Scroll down to the bottom of the page to the table "Comparison of State Ranks." Examine the rankings for the past several years. In particular, track rankings 1–3 and 49–51. Why do you think the states in these positions have changed? What conditions could account for a state dropping from #1 to #10, as in the case of Iowa between 1998 and 1999? What may a state have done to raise its ranking? Select a state with a high rank and one with a very low rank. Research specific conditions that may help to explain the status of children in each state. In the case of a state with a low ranking, are there particular groups within the state that are more disadvantaged or are conditions widespread?

34. ANCESTRY IN THE UNITED STATES

Site address: http://www.census.gov/population/www/ancestry.html

Type of data: statistical data sets

Key terms: immigration; ancestry; foreign born; median age; cultural landscape

GEOGRAPHIC CONTEXT

The story of the United States is a story of *immigration*. Because, at different points in time, immigrants have come from virtually all parts of the world, the fabric of our national *ancestry* is rich and varied. Not every group has had the same experience after settling here, however. The U.S. Census Bureau gathers data on selected characteristics according ancestry. These files allow comparison and analysis of 70 ancestry groups in terms of such characteristics as education, use of English language, income, and economic activity.

THINKING CRITICALLY

Open the "Ancestry" page of the U.S. Census Bureau site.

1. Scroll down to "1990 Census: Profiles of Our Ancestry." Select "English." What percent of the total population in 1990 was of English ancestry? What percent of these people were born in the United States? Create a profile of the population of English ancestry, including such characteristics as education, occupation, and income.

2. Scroll down to Table 5 "Population for Selected Ancestry Groups." What ancestry groups have populations of more than one million people? What groups have populations with more than 50 percent *foreign born*? What is the *median age* of the population in each ancestry group? Present this information graphically. Lead a class discussion about ancestry patterns in the United States. How is ancestry reflected in the *cultural landscape* (landscape as altered by human groups) of the country?

3. Scroll down to Table 5 "Population for Selected Ancestry Groups." Identify the top ten ancestry groups in terms of percent who entered the United States between 1980 and 1990. What circumstances prompted these groups to immigrate to the United States? Research conditions in the countries of origin to determine what factors may have contributed to the decision to leave. Create a bulletin board display based on your research. What generalizations can you make about migration today?

4. Explore the question: "Do population groups that are primarily foreign born have a different demographic profile than groups that are primarily born in the United States?" Use data in Table 5 "Population for Selected Ancestry Groups" to select two groups for study, for example, Nigerians and Germans. Examine the data for each group? What data have you chosen for comparison? Why? Are there categories for which the contrast is surprising? Why? What generalizations can you make? Are generalizations based on the analysis of only two groups sound? How can you test your conclusions?

35. SELECTED HISTORICAL U.S. CENSUS DATA: FOREIGN-BORN POPULATION

Site address: http://www.census.gov/population/www/censusdata/pop-hc.html

Select: "Historical Census Statistics on the Foreign-Born Population of the United States: 1850 to 1990"

Type of data: census data set

Key terms: immigrant flows; scale; population characteristics

GEOGRAPHIC CONTEXT

The population of the United States is largely the product of historical migration waves that have introduced a broad diversity of people, cultures, and customs into the country. Over time the numbers and points of origin of immigrants have varied but the trend and its evolving impact on the cultural landscape of the country have persisted. Decennial census (census collected every ten years as mandated by the Constitution) records, maintained by the U.S. Bureau of the Census, provide a window on who these immigrants were and the places from which they came in the period 1850–1990.

THINKING CRITICALLY

1. Select Table 1. "Nativity of the Population and Place of Birth of the Native Population: 1850 to 1990." Examine the census data and look for patterns in *immigrant flows*. Consider ways in which the data can best be represented in order to illustrate major periods in immigration history, for example, a thematic map to show flow; a complex line graph to show numbers.

2. Select Table 4. "Region and Country or Area of Birth of the Foreign-Born Population, With Geographic Detail Shown in Decennial Census Publications of 1930 or Earlier: 1850 to 1930 and 1960 to 1990." Geographers are always concerned with the ways in which *scale* (degree of generalization) affects the understanding of places and data about those places. Compare the data presented in Table 1 with that in Table 4 and consider the role of scale in data analysis. How does the generalization of data in Table 1 influence the understanding of the immigration history of the United States?

3. Select Table 7. "Age and Sex of the Foreign-Born Population: 1870 to 1990." Use data from this table to construct population pyramids for the immigrant populations to the United States. What *population characteristics* distinguish the immigrant population over the years? Have these characteristics changed over time? Develop a rationale for the characteristics observed.

4. Select Table 18. "Nativity of the Population by Urban-Rural Residence and Size of Place: 1870 to 1940 and 1960 to 1990." What patterns can be observed about the destinations of immigrants to the United States? How do you account for such patterns? Assume you are an immigrant to the United States in one of the following years: 1870; 1910; 1960; 1990. Write a letter to your cousin in your native homeland describing your life in the United States.

36. SELECTED HISTORICAL U.S. CENSUS DATA: POPULATION OF URBAN PLACES

Site address: http://www.census.gov/population/www/censusdata/pop-hc.html

Select: "Population of the 100 Largest Cities and Other Urban Places in the United States: 1790 to 1990"

Type of data: statistical data set

Key terms: city; urbanized area; graduated point symbol; pattern; population trend

GEOGRAPHIC CONTEXT

While at the time of the first census in 1790 only about five percent of the population lived in urban places, today more than three-quarters of the U.S. population live in urban places. The growth and spread of urban places, therefore, offers insight into the changing lifestyles of the U.S. population. Just as the population has slowly shifted first west and more recently southwest, so too have the largest cities followed this trend. The earliest cities were concentrated in the northeast but now the greatest growth is occurring in the cities of the south and west. Such changes and patterns are of particular interest to population and urban geographers. The U.S. Bureau of the Census maintains population data for urban places.

THINKING CRITICALLY

1. On the document main page, scroll down and select Text Table B. "Population of the 20 Largest Cities and Urbanized Areas: 1990." Note that the rankings vary between *city* and *urbanized area*. What is the difference? Why does the Census Bureau make this distinction? Create two maps, locating on one the cities and on the other the urbanized areas. Use *graduated point symbols* to indicate relative size. What pattern is revealed in the distribution of major cities? What does this suggest about the U.S. population?

2. On the document main page, scroll down and select Table 2. "Population of 24 Urban Places: 1790." Make a map on which you locate and show relative

size of each urban place on the list for 1790. Now repeat this process with Table 12. "Population of the 100 Largest Urban Places: 1890," mapping only the top 30 urban places. Finally make a map based on Table 22. "Population of the 100 Largest Urban Places: 1990," again mapping only the top 30 places. Analyze the maps you have made and describe the patterns you observe. Apply your knowledge of U.S. history to explain the patterns.

3. On the document main page, scroll down and select Table 25. "Distribution of the . . . Largest Urban Places, by Section and Subsection of the United States: 1790–1990." Analyze the data in this table and decide on the most appropriate graphing format to present it. In which region is your state? Where does your region fall in this *pattern*? Is your region gaining or losing population?

4. On the document main page, scroll down and select Table 1. "Rank by Population of the 100 Largest Urban Places, Listed Alphabetically by State: 1790–1990." Select your state and several others, for example, Pennsylvania, Ohio, Texas, Arizona, and California. Analyze the city rankings over this 200-year period. Select one or two representative cities from each state. Locate them on a map of the United States. Then create graphs that show *population trends* in terms of rank. Refer to Table 23 to determine when each city was at its peak population. Use the data, map, and graphs you have collected and constructed as the basis for a report to the governor of your state in which you discuss the history of urban growth in the United States from 1790 to 1990 and the significance of historical trends for your state. What is the significance of the trends revealed in the map and graphs for your state?

37. U.S. IMMIGRATION & NATURALIZATION STATISTICS

Site address: http://www.ins.usdoj.gov/graphics/aboutins/statistics/index. htm

Type of data: statistical data sets

Key terms: immigrant; cultural landscape; illegal alien

GEOGRAPHIC CONTEXT

The human geography of the United States has been shaped largely by a succession of *immigrants* who have brought with them customs, languages, foods, religions, attitudes, and values that have merged to form the American *cultural landscape* (landscape as altered by human groups). The flow of immigrants has varied over the years in response to changing world events and conditions within the United States. In addition some states have attracted more immigrants than others, contributing to a patchwork pattern of diverse people across the country. The Immigration and Naturalization Service (INS) maintains records of immigrants to the United States.

THINKING CRITICALLY

1. On the "INS" main page, select "Immigration to the United States in Fiscal Year 1996." Then select "Characteristics of Legal Immigrants." Read this narrative summary of immigrant characteristics and convert the statistical facts into a graphic presentation that profiles immigration to the United States in 1996. For example, where did most immigrants end up? Who were they? What did they do?

2. On the "INS" main page, select "Illegal Alien Resident Population." Then select Table 1. Create maps that show the main countries of origin of *illegal aliens* and the main destination states within the United States of those illegal immigrants. Analyze the patterns and speculate on what conditions compel people to leave their countries and what attractions draw them to particular states. Research U.S. immigration laws and penalties that apply to illegal aliens.

3. On the "INS" main page, select "Immigration Fact Sheet." Scroll down and select "Country of Origin." Create maps and graphs that show the "Top Ten Countries of Birth" for 1996, for 1981–96, and for 1820–1996. As you change the scale of the data, how does the overall pattern change? Scroll down through the table to locate data on the top ten countries from which tourists visited the United States in 1996. Do the same for students studying in the United States. Convert this data into maps or graphs. How does this flow of people from other countries affect American culture? Look for examples of immigrant influence in your community.

4. On the "INS" main page, select "Immigration Fact Sheet." Scroll down and select "State and Metropolitan Area of Residence." Create a choropleth map of the United States that shows the states with the largest populations of immigrants in 1996. Then add to the map graduated point symbols indicating those metropolitan areas attracting the most immigrants in 1996. On separate maps show those states receiving the most refugees and those with the most illegal aliens. What patterns do you see in these maps? What is the attraction of these states to immigrants?

38. U.S. CENSUS BUREAU: INTERNATIONAL DATA BASE

Site address: http://www.census.gov/ipc/www/idbnew.html

Type of data: statistical data sets; graphics

Key terms: diversity; demography; socio-economic conditions; age structure; cohort; population pyramid; aggregation; projection; estimate

GEOGRAPHIC CONTEXT

With more than 200 countries and 6 billion people, the world is a complex and diverse place. *Diversity* is more than cultural differences; it

also includes patterns in *demography* (scientific study of human populations) and *socio-economic conditions*. Countries can be compared, for
example, in terms of populations, vital rates, migration, literacy, or employment. Comparison is the first step in the analytical process that leads
to a better understanding of how and why some countries prosper while
others struggle to meet the daily needs of their people. Such questions
are a central concern to population geographers. The Census Bureau's
International Data Base (IDB) includes selected data for 227 countries
and areas from 1950 to the present and projected to 2050.

THINKING CRITICALLY

1. On the "IDB" main page, select "Summary Demographic Data." In the drop-
   down country menu, select a country, for example Afghanistan, and "submit
   query." Analyze the summary data for Afghanistan in order to create a demographic profile of the country. Consider such factors as growth trends and
   age structure (proportion of males and females in each age category). Compare
   current and projected indicators. Account for the period of negative growth
   between 1980 and 1990. Create a set of graphs that portray a demographic
   picture of Afghanistan.

2. On the "IDB" main page, select "Online Access" and "Display." From the first
   drop-down menu, select Table 004. "Enumerated and Adjusted Population,
   by Age and Sex." From the second drop-down menu select a country, for
   example, Canada. Choose a time period, for example, "Latest available year"
   and "Submit Query." Use this data, presented in 5-year age/sex *cohorts*, to
   construct a *population pyramid* (a graph showing the distribution of population
   by age and sex). Analyze the pyramid in order to speculate on social and
   economic conditions in Canada.

3. On the "IDB" main page, select "Online Demographic *Aggregation*." Select
   Table 008. "Vital Rates and Events" and "Display Mode." Then select the type
   of data you want to examine, for example, "rates," "treat each region sepa-
   rately," "aggregate region data," "less developed and more developed countries," and "latest available year." "Submit query" and analyze the results. On
   the basis of the data available, formulate definitions that distinguish less developed countries from more developed countries. Experiment with aggre-
   gating the data in different ways to test your definitions.

4. On the "IDB" main page, select "Population Pyramids." Select a country, for
   example Costa Rica, and "Summary" output. "Submit Query" and analyze
   the current and *projected* population pyramids. Describe the changes expected
   in Costa Rica's population structure. Access pyramids for Kenya. Compare
   these pyramids with those of Costa Rica. How do you account for the differences? Access additional data from the International Data Base to test your
   hypotheses about these two countries.

5. On the "IDB" main page, select "World Population Information." Select
   "Historical Estimates of World Population." Examine these estimates of pop-

ulation from 10,000 B.C. to 1950. Summarize the general trends and compare the *estimates* from different sources. Why is there so much variation in the estimates? Evaluate the sources of data used to compile the table. Construct a graph of world population over time and justify the choices you have made.

Additional international demographic data sites:

United Nations Statistical Division: Demographic Yearbook (38a)
http://www.un.org/Depts/unsd/demog/index.html
Revision of the World Population Estimates and Projections (UN) (38b)
http://www.popin.org/pop1998/
Population Reference Bureau (38c)
http://www.prb.org

39. UNITED NATIONS STATISTICS DIVISION: SOCIAL INDICATORS

Site address: http://www.un.org/Depts/unsd/social/main.htm

Type of data: statistical data sets

Key terms: quality of life; social indicators; sex ratio; life expectancy; infant mortality rate; age structure

GEOGRAPHIC CONTEXT

Quality of life can be evaluated by comparing and analyzing a variety of *social indicators*, including among others such topics as population, water supply and sanitation, health, education and income, and economic activity. Individual countries can be profiled and studied, or selected countries can be compared in terms of one or more indicators. The United Nations maintains a global statistical database drawn from national and international sources.

THINKING CRITICALLY

Open the "UN Social Indicators" main page.

1. Select "Population." The ratio of males to females (per 100) in a population is known as *sex ratio*. There are typically more females than males in a population. Scan the data for the countries of the world. Make a list of those countries in which there are more than 100 males for every 100 females. Consider the countries on your list. What characteristics do these countries share? Form a hypothesis about countries with a high proportion of males. How can you test this hypothesis?

2. Select "Health." Use the data in the table to answer the question: Is there a correlation between *life expectancy* at birth and *infant mortality rate*? What is your conclusion? Are there exceptions? Select 20 representative countries from the list and make graphs or choropleth maps that show your findings. Then explain what you have learned to the class.

3. Select "Education." Examine the data for variations in "expected number of years of formal schooling." What is the range? Identify the top and bottom ten countries. Locate these countries on a map. What are some consequences for a country of limited formal education? Make a list of social and economic indicators that you consider good measures of development. Research the countries you have identified? Does there seem to be a correlation between education and development? Write an advocacy statement in support of basic education based on your findings.

4. Select "Youth and elderly population." The *age structure* (proportion of males and females in each age category) of a population may provide clues to the overall quality of life in a country. Scan the data for percent of total population under age 15 and percent of male and female populations aged 60 and over. What are some implications of a "young" population, that is, one in which a high percent of the total population is under age 15? What is suggested if the percent of population aged 60 and over is very small? What issues are presented by an "aging" population? Find examples of each of these situations. Use additional data from the UN Social Indicators site to develop a profile of these countries. Draft a 5-year action plan for each country, recommending steps that will be necessary to meet the needs of the population in the future.

40. HUMAN DEVELOPMENT REPORT 1998

Site address: http://www.undp.org/hdro/

Type of data: statistical data sets

Key terms: level of development; quality of life; development indicators; development index

GEOGRAPHIC CONTEXT

Countries vary greatly, not just in terms of culture or language, but also in terms of *level of development* and *quality of life*. There is no single basis for measuring development. The concept itself is subjective and the focus of much disagreement. In an effort to present the multiple faces of development, the United Nations Development Programme publishes an annual "Human Development Report" (HDR) in which *development indicators* and selected *indices* for ranking countries on the basis of their development are presented. Both the indicators and the indices provide rich opportunities for critical analysis.

THINKING CRITICALLY

1. An *index* is a ranking based on a composite assessment of selected indicators. On the "HDR" main page, select "Human Development Report 1998" and then "About the indices." What indicators are the basis for the "Human Development Index" and the "Gender-related Development Index"? Evaluate the indicators selected? Why do you think these particular indicators were selected? What do you think would happen if the indicators were changed? Create your own "development index." Be sure to justify each indicator selected in terms of what it measures. Test your index by using "Statistics" accessible from the HDR main page.

2. On the "HDR" main page, select "Human Development Report 1998" and then "Human Development Index (HDI)." Note the HDI rankings. Now select the "Gender-related Development Index" and compare the rankings of this index with those of the Human Development Index. Identify several countries in which there is a variation in rank of more than 5. What does this suggest about built-in bias in any system of ranking? Does this make indexing a meaningless exercise? Debate the value of indexing as a measure of development.

3. On the "HDR" main page, select "HDRs 1990–1997" and then select "Human Development Report 1996." Compare the HDI rankings in 1996 with those of 1998. Which countries moved up or down? Select several of these countries and research the circumstances that might account for the shift in rank. Note that the United States dropped from second to fourth position. Examine the indicators to develop an explanation for this decline.

4. On the "HDR" main page, scroll to the bottom of the page and select "National Human Development Reports" (NHDR). Select "List of Reports" and then navigate through "Europe and the Commonwealth of Independent States" to "Kazakhstan" to "Summary of 1996 NHDR." Use the maps, tables, and narrative to develop a descriptive poster that summarizes the status of human well-being in this country. What indicators will you emphasize? What issues are most urgent? How can you evaluate the information found?

41. CENSUS OF INDIA

Site address: http://censusindia.net/

Type of data: statistical data set; maps; graphs

Key terms: census; spatial analysis; population growth; natural increase; migration; density

GEOGRAPHIC CONTEXT

A national *census* presents a detailed picture of a country at a particular point in time. The data collected supports *spatial analysis* (a type of geographical analysis that attempts to explain patterns and distributions of phenomena) within the country as well as the study of trends over time. With a population second only to that of China, India is an important country that needs to be studied and understood. The "Census of India" includes a broad variety of data sets, maps, and graphs that reveal patterns and trends in this unique country.

THINKING CRITICALLY

Open the "Census of India" main page.

1. Select "India at a Glance." Then select "Variation in Population Since 1901." Create graphs that show the change in India's total population, as well as changes in rural and urban populations. Calculate and graph rates of change. Use your graphs to explain how *population growth* is the result of *natural increase* (births minus deaths) and *migration*.

2. Select "India at a Glance." Use the data under "Work Participation Rate," "Religions," and "Languages Spoken" to create a set of graphs that show key social and economic characteristics of India's population. How have employment structure and cultural diversity affected India's development? Plan an interview with an "average" person in India. What questions would you ask? What characteristics and conditions most likely define that person's life?

3. Select "Census Data," "Census Data Online," and "Main Menu." From this menu select "General Data" and "Table 3: Density, Per cent Decadal Variation, 1991." On a map of India with state boundaries, create a choropleth map showing patterns of population *density*. Is India's population evenly distributed? What factors might account for the distribution patterns? Use maps in an atlas to explore this question.

4. Select "Census Data," "Census Data Online," and "Main Menu." From this menu select "Literacy and Education" and "Table 14: Literary Rate by Sex in States and Union Territories, 1991." Use the data in this table to evaluate variations in the level of education in India. In particular, note variations among states, between males and females, and between rural and urban areas. How might these education patterns affect India's level of development? What do they suggest about the status of women in India? Locate the data for the southern state of Kerala. What is unusual about this state? Refer to other tables in "Census Data Online" to develop a profile of the state of Kerala. Conduct further research to try to account for Kerala's statistics compared to the rest of India.

42. CANADIAN STATISTICS

Site address: http://www.statcan.ca:80/english/Pgdb/

Type of data: statistical data sets

Key terms: population growth; trade balance; political parties; age structure

GEOGRAPHIC CONTEXT

The United States and Canada are neighbors and share many common characteristics. However, each is unique in many respects. It is possible to construct a profile of Canada using data from the government of Canada national census. In addition, such data reveal the great diversity among Canada's provinces and territories.

THINKING CRITICALLY

Open the "Canadian Statistics" main page.

1. Select "Population." On the next page, select "Population" again, and then "Population and growth components, 1851–1996." Construct a series of graphs that show the development of Canada's population overtime. When were periods of peak growth? What factors contributed to that growth? Compare the growth of the Canadian population to the growth of the population in the United States ([42a] http://www.census.gov).

2. Select "International Trade." On the next page select "International Trade" again and then "Imports, exports and trade balance of goods. . . ." Evaluate Canada's trade position in recent years. Who are Canada's main trade partners? Is the *trade balance* (exports minus imports) positive or negative? Represent this information on a map. Now access the tables showing exports and imports by products. Which areas of production contribute to Canada's negative trade balance with some regions?

3. Select "Government." Then select "Elections" and "Distribution of House of Commons seats. . . ." How many *political parties* held seats in the House of Commons in the most recent election? On a map of Canada with provincial and territorial boundaries, show the distribution of party representation. Which parties are widely represented? Which parties seem to be localized in their support? Research one of the localized parties to find out why it is popular in only certain places? Are there similar parties in the United States?

4. Select "Population." On the next page, select "Population" again, and then "Population by sex and age, Canada, the provinces and territories." Scroll down to see the percent distribution of population by age and sex for the country and for each province or territory. (Use the drop-down menu above the table to see additional provinces.) Construct graphs to show the *age structure* (proportion of males and females in each age category) of Canada and each province or territory. Which provinces or territories vary from the national average? Use additional resources to investigate why some provinces or territories have a larger or smaller percent of the population in a particular group. Does the United States have similar variations among the states? Visit the U.S. Census Bureau site ([42a] http://www.census.gov) to find out about age structure in the United States.

43. FEDERAL STATISTICAL OFFICE GERMANY

Site address: http://www.statistik-bund.de/e_home.htm

Type of data: census data

Key terms: population pyramid; growth rate; immigrant patterns; trade; trade balance; wages; exchange rate

GEOGRAPHIC CONTEXT

A census is a picture of a population at a given point in time. Historical census data allows comparison and analysis of trends. A cross-section of census data provides a better understanding of the social and economic dynamics of a country. Geographers use census data, such as that gathered by the government of Germany, to learn about people and places.

THINKING CRITICALLY

Open the "Federal Statistical Office Germany" main page and select "Figures and Facts."

1. Select "Basic data" and "Population." Read the text summary, then select "Graphs" from the sidebar. Select the "Population Pyramid" (a graph that shows distribution of population by age and sex). Interpret the graph. How can you account for the bulges and dips in population over time? Speculate on the current *growth rate* (births minus deaths plus/minus migration) of the German population. Now select the graph "Annual increase and decrease in population." Relate this graph to the population pyramid.

2. Select "Basic data" and "Population." From the sidebar, select "Tables." Construct a graphic profile of the German population in terms of citizenship. On a world map, locate the source countries for the major foreign groups residing in Germany. Use graduated flow lines to show the *immigrant patterns*. Research factors that might account for the presence of these groups in Germany.

3. Select "Basic data" and "External trade." From the sidebar, select "Tables." Who are Germany's main *trade* partners? What are the main trade items? Compare exports and imports. Based on this information, speculate on Germany's *trade balance* (exports minus imports).

4. Select "Basic data" and "Wages and salaries." From the sidebar, select "Tables." Select an activity, for example, production industries. Compare the *wages* and hours worked by males and females. How does Germany compare to the United States? Research the current *exchange rate* (value of currency relative to the U.S. dollar) on the German mark. How do wages in Germany compare to wages in the United States? Create a poster on which you compare wages and salaries in Germany and the United States.

44. WOMEN OF THE WORLD

Site address: http://www.un.org/womenwatch/world/index.html

Type of data: statistical data sets; government documents

Key terms: aggregate; status of women; national action plan; empowerment of women

GEOGRAPHIC CONTEXT

Women make up slightly less than half of the world's population. Their special needs are often overlooked in favor of *aggregate* needs of the total population or needs that are particular to men. The *status of women* is often significantly inferior to that of men, especially in many less developed countries of the world. Following several global conferences devoted to issues related to women, awareness of women's rights and needs has been raised. Nevertheless, great disparity exists among the countries of the world. The United Nations has directed special attention to the *status of women* through its program on the Advancement and Empowerment of Women and its Internet site "WomenWatch." Following the global conference on women in Beijing in 1995, United Nations member countries were called upon to draft strategies and *national action plans* to improve the status of women in their respective countries. Progress has been varied, reflecting both cultural and economic circumstances.

THINKING CRITICALLY

Open the "Women of the World" main page.

1. One avenue to *empowerment of women* is access to education. Select "Africa" and "Statistics." Scroll down to Section 4 and select "Illiteracy rate by sex." Scan the data to determine a general trend for the region. How do women compare to men in terms of illiteracy? Are there any indications of improvement? (Note the rates for women over 25 years of age. How is this a clue to past access to education?) Identify several countries in which female illiteracy is particularly higher than male illiteracy. What factors may contribute to this disparity? What are some consequences of such disparity? Select one country and research the status of women in depth.

2. Select "Asia and the Pacific" and "Statistics." Scroll down to Section 3 and select "Life expectancy and infant mortality rate." Scan the data. Return to Section 3 and select "Births attended and maternal mortality." Scan the data. In both tables note the statistics listed for Israel and Japan. Based on these statistics, how would you rate the *status of women* in these two countries? Why? How do other countries of Asia compare? In which countries is the

status of women similar? In which countries do women fair worse? Look for patterns in the data? What additional information do you need in order to account for differences in the status of women among the countries of Asia? Write a position paper for presentation at the next World Conference on Women.

3. In the sidebar, select "Statistics and Indicators." Select "Women in parliament: percent of women in each National Parliament." Construct two world-level choropleth maps showing the percent of women in the Lower House of the government and the percent in the Upper House. Analyze the patterns. Based on your maps, where do women have the greatest voice in national decision-making? Use data available within the site to address the question: Is the general status of women higher in those countries in which women have greater voice?

4. In the sidebar, select "Follow-up to Beijing." Then select "Links to: National level" and "National plans of action." The World Conference on Women in Beijing in 1995 called upon all governments to develop action plans to address the needs of women. From the list of *national action plans* available online, select representative countries from around the world. (Note: some action plans may not be available in English.) Study the action plans. Then convene a mock Conference on Women to present, debate, and defend the plans pro-posed by each country represented. Conclude the conference by drafting a "Universal Bill of Women's Rights."

45. UNITED NATIONS HIGH COMMISSION FOR REFUGEES

Site address: http://www.unhcr.ch/

Type of data: statistical data sets

Key terms: refugee; internally displaced person; countries of origin; countries of asylum; age structure

GEOGRAPHIC CONTEXT

Refugees and *internally displaced persons* are terms used to define a broad group of people who have been granted temporary or permanent pro-tection on humanitarian grounds. While refugees, are most often asso-ciated with political conflict or war, they also may be people fleeing from conditions of extreme economic or environmental stress. The United Nations High Commission for Refugees (UNHCR) attempts to monitor both international and intra-national movements of people. UNHCR pro-vides assistance in meeting basic needs and in repatriation for those without access to other resources. UNHCR reports on the plight of ref-ugees through its Internet site "RefWorld."

THINKING CRITICALLY

Open the "UNHCR" main page.

1. Select "UNHCR and Refugees" and read background information available on this page. Prepare a public information speech in which you explain the different types of refugees, the role of UNHCR in meeting their needs, and some of the problems associated with gathering accurate information about refugee groups. Present your speech to the class and invite discussion.
2. Select "Statistics" and "A Statistical Overview (July 1999)." Then select "Table I.2 Refugee population by country of asylum and orgin, 1997–1998." Compare the numbers of total refugees and those who were "UNHCR assisted" for 1997 and 1998. Analyze the differences and speculate on the implications of UNHCR non-involvement with certain groups.
3. Select "Statistics" and "A Statistical Overview (July 1999)." Then select "Table I.2 Refugee population by country of asylum and origin, 1997–1998." Create a series of regional maps showing major refugee flows between *countries of origin* and *countries of asylum*. Which countries have the greatest level of refugee activity. What conditions have caused these people to flee their countries? What are some implications for countries of asylum? Select one country from the list and research conditions in that country. Write a newspaper article reporting your findings.
4. Select "Statistics" and "A Statistical Overview (July 1999)." Then select "Table III.1 UNHCR assisted refugees by gender and age, 1998." Scan the data and analyze the general *age structure* of most refugee populations. What groups (i.e., age, sex) are most likely to become refugees? Choose several countries for closer scrutiny and compare the general demographic characteristics in Table III.1 with the other tables on the site. Summarize your findings in a poster that creates a profile of refugees in general. Why is it important that such information be collected? How do governments and international organizations use this data?

46. STATISTICAL HIGHLIGHTS OF U.S. AGRICULTURE

Site address: http://www.usda.gov/nass/pubs/stathigh/1999/sthi98-c.htm
Type of data: statistical data sets; maps
Key terms: labor force; production; yield

GEOGRAPHIC CONTEXT

Agriculture has been an important part of the U.S. economy throughout the country's history. Until around the turn of the twentieth century, more than half of the country's *labor force* was engaged in agriculture. While today only a very small percent of the labor force remains engaged in agriculture, this primary activity continues to be an important part of the national productive output. Because of the country's size and variety of soils and climates, agricultural production varies widely, ranging from staple grains to fruits and vegetables. The National Agricultural Statistics Service (NASS) of the Department of Agriculture records data related to crops in the United States.

THINKING CRITICALLY

Open the "NASS" main page.

1. Select "Value of Crop Production." Create a graph that shows the value of crop *production* in the United States from 1993 to 1998. What trend do you observe? Which category of crops has the greatest value? What role does agriculture play in your local economy? Why do agriculture prices fluctuate? What impact does fluctuation in agricultural prices have on your family?

2. Select "Top 5 States for Selected Commodities." Create a thematic map showing the major producing areas for these commodities. What patterns of production do you see? Why are these states major agriculture producers? Research what percent of the population in these states is engaged in agriculture (see [42a] http://www.census.gov). What effect does agriculture have on average incomes?

3. In the sidebar, select "Agricultural Graphics." Under "Crops" select "Field Crops." Select and print the map for "Corn Acreage" and for "Corn Yield." Use the statistics shown on the maps to create choropleth maps. Repeat this process for several other crops, for example, soybeans and winter wheat. Compare the maps and formulate some generalization about production of these crops in the United States? Why do certain states produce more of a particular crop than others? What physical and human factors influence decisions affecting agriculture production?

4. In the sidebar, select "Agricultural Graphics." Under "Crops" select "County Maps." Access the crop "Yield Maps" for 1998 for corn, oats, soybeans, and wheat. Describe the patterns revealed on the maps. What factors influence these patterns? Compare these maps with maps from an earlier year? Can any changes be observed? Why? Why not?

47. CGIAR: CONSULTATIVE GROUP ON INTERNATIONAL AGRICULTURAL RESEARCH

Site address: http://www.cgiar.org
Type of data: photographs; narrative discussion
Key terms: production; consumption; staple crop

GEOGRAPHIC CONTEXT

Agriculture accounts for a large percent of the labor force in many countries around the world, particularly in less developed countries. Research in agriculture plays an important role in meeting the food needs of the world's ever growing population. Agriculturally productive land is unevenly distributed around the world and as a result, crop production varies widely, depending on soil, climate, economic conditions, and cultural preferences. The Consultative Group on International Agricultural Research (CGIAR) promotes agricultural development through programs of research, education, and policy support.

THINKING CRITICALLY

Open the "CGIAR" main page.

1. Select "CGIAR Photos." Select different crop varieties listed in the "CGIAR photo gallery." Observe plant characteristics, growing conditions and problems, and locations. In particular look at crops with which you are not familiar. Record your observations in a chart. Then research selected crops to determine the distribution of *production* and *consumption*. Which crops are staples for large populations? What role does plant research play in meeting global food needs?

2. Select "CGIAR Research" and then "Areas of Research." Under "Cereals," select "Wheat." Read the passage and extract key points in order to make a poster about wheat production and consumption, its uses, and its nutritional value. How has research improved this *staple crop*? Research wheat production in the United States. Where and what varieties are produced here?

3. Select "CGIAR Research" and then "Areas of Research." Under "Cereals," select "Rice." Read the passage on rice and then access the link to "Riceweb" (near the end of the passage or go directly to [47a] http://www.cgiar.org/irri/Riceweb/Contents.htm). On the "RICEWEB" main page, select "begin here . . ." Then select "Feeding the World" and "Facts and Figures." Under "Rice production," select each region to obtain a profile of rice production, land area, and yield. Represent this data in a series of maps or graphs that show the distribution of rice production worldwide. Identify which countries have the greatest absolute production and which have the greatest per hectare yield. Return to the "Rice Facts Index" and compare these countries in terms of overall agricultural production, trade, and general demographic characteristics. Is there a typical profile of a rice-producing country?

4. Select "CGIAR Research," "Areas of Research,"and then select each crop under "Roots, Tubers, Banana and Plantain." These crops provide the staple diet in many tropical regions of the world. Read each passage, collecting basic information. Then do further research to determine distribution, production, and consumption of these crops. Present your findings through maps and graphs. Visit an ethnic supermarket, if one is available. Purchase and sample any of these basic root crops with which you are not familiar.

5. Contact the state agriculture office to learn more about food production in your state. What types of crops are produced? Do farmers use new varieties that are the result of research conducted by CGIAR or similar organizations?

48. OFFICE OF TRADE AND ECONOMIC ANALYSIS

Site address: http://www.ita.doc.gov/td/industry/otea/

Type of data: statistical data sets

Key terms: global economy; export; import; net trade balance; trade deficit; commodity; flow map

GEOGRAPHIC CONTEXT

The United States is a major player in the *global economy*. Knowing and understanding patterns of trade is critical to the country's economic well-being. Trade can be categorized into two major divisions: domestic and international. Some states are more actively engaged in international trade than others, giving them a comparative economic advantage. Over time U.S. trade patterns have changed, both in terms of goods traded and trading partners. The Office of Trade and Economic Analysis (OTEA) in the U.S. Department of Commerce maintains a comprehensive database of trade statistics.

THINKING CRITICALLY

Open the "OTEA" main page.

1. Scroll down and select "U.S. Foreign Trade Highlights" and then "U.S. Aggregate Foreign Trade Data." Now select Table 3. "U.S. Trade in Goods, 1972–98." Examine the *aggregate* trade statistics and decide on an appropriate method of graphic presentation that shows trends in *exports, imports,* and *net trade balance* (exports minus imports) in the United States between 1972 and 1998. Which categories of goods have been most dynamic? Which categories have contributed most to the U.S. *trade deficit* (import expenditures in excess of export earnings)? Assume you work for the U.S. Department of Commerce. Write a speech for presentation to Congress on the "State of the Nation's Trade."

2. Scroll down and select "U.S. Foreign Trade Highlights" and then "U.S. Aggregate Foreign Trade Data." Now select Table 10. "Top 50 Purchasers of U.S. Exports" and Table 11. "Top 50 Suppliers of U.S. Imports." Create maps that show main U.S. trade partners, one for exports and another for imports. Research the types of products traded. Select one country that appears on both maps and convene mock trade negotiations. Consider such topics as trade balances, tariff agreements, and access to markets.

3. Scroll down and select "U.S. Foreign Trade Highlights" and then "U.S. Commodity Trade by World and Regions." Select two contrasting world regions,

for example, South America and Western Europe. Make a chart of the top 20 export *commodities* and the top 20 import commodities for each region. Compare and contrast the types of goods traded. How can you account for differences? What characteristics of any given region influence the nature of U.S. trade with that region?

4. Scroll down and select "State Export Data." Scroll down to "Export Markets for Each State" and select your state from the drop-down menu. Create a *flow map* (a map showing the movement of trade by means of a line, the width of which is proportional to the volume of trade) that shows the top 20 export markets for your state, indicating value of trade. Research your state's trade. What commodities does the state export? What share of your state's annual income comes from export trade? Write a letter to your governor addressing the importance of trade to the state's economy.

5. Make a survey of products in your home, both durable goods and perishable items. Record the point of origin of each item and create a map showing the source of items you use each day. How would your life be affected if all foreign trade were to cease?

49. CITIES OF TODAY, CITIES OF TOMORROW

Site address: http://www.un.org/Pubs/CyberSchoolBus/special/habitat/index.html

Type of data: narrative; statistical data; photographs

Key terms: urban; urban place; urbanization; city; urban problems; city profile

GEOGRAPHIC CONTEXT

The world's population is becoming increasingly *urban*, with almost three-quarter of the people of Europe and North and South America living in *urban places*. The populations of Asia and Africa are *urbanizing* rapidly, as well. Cities pose special challenges to the people living there, including such issues as quality of life, health, employment, transportation, and pollution. These and other problems are of particular interest to urban geographers. The United Nations CyberSchoolBus program presents a wide array of UN data through six teaching units focusing on cities.

THINKING CRITICALLY

Open the "Cities" main page and select "Table of Contents."

1. Think about the word "city." What images come to mind? Write a definition of the word. Then from the "Table of Contents," select "Unit 1: What is a City?" and "Text." Read the passage about "urban definition." What are some

problems in defining the word "city"? Did you encounter some of these problems as you wrote your definition? Read the rest of the passage. Then navigate to the "Activities" and use these questions to lead a class discussion. How does urban development in your state compare with that occurring on a global scale?

2. From the "Table of Contents," select "Unit 3: What is a City Made Of?" and "Text." Read the passage "How a city works. . . ." What *problems* are associated with urban places? How many of these problems affect urban places in your state? Select the link "high population density" and compare the data in the two columns of Table 4. Research similar data for your state. Use the links provided to learn about problems associated with water and garbage services. Extract the statistics cited and construct a chart that summarizes the main issues.

3. From the "Table of Contents," select "Unit 5: Consequences of Urbanization" and "Text." Read the passage; then navigate to "Activities." Use the questions provided to explore problems associated with urbanization. Use the information provided plus ideas that emerge during discussion to form your own position: Are cities places of "urban doom" or are they "crucibles of cultural, economic, and social development"?

4. From the "Cities" main page, select "City Profiles." Select several *city profiles*, for example, Abidjan, Berlin, Rio de Janeiro, and Toronto. Compare these cities representing different major world regions. What characteristics do they have in common? In what ways are they different? How does reliance on just these profiles limit your ability to evaluate the urban conditions of each of these cities. Research additional UN databases to expand these city profiles; then reconsider your comparisons.

50. NIGHTTIME LIGHTS OF THE WORLD

Site address: http://julius.ngdc.noaa.gov:8080/production/html/BIOMASS/night. html

Type of data: satellite-based digital map

Key terms: composite image; pattern; settlement pattern; population density; economic development

GEOGRAPHIC CONTEXT

The technology of satellites and computers has provided us with an array of new ways of viewing Earth. *Composite images* are created by merging data from multiple sources to create a single view of Earth. Nighttime human activity almost always involves some type of light source that can be captured by special satellite-mounted cameras. Light sources may be towns and cities, rural villages, fires, or oil field burn-off. The composite "Nighttime Lights" map of the world, provided by the National Oceanographic and Atmospheric Administration (NOAA), is a unique way to study the distribution of human populations and activities.

THINKING CRITICALLY

1. Examine the "Nighttime Lights" map of the world. Describe the *patterns* visible on the map and create a list of places of especially high concentration. Use maps in an atlas to identify physical and human characteristics of the areas of high concentration on the Nighttime Lights map. What generalizations can you make about human *settlement patterns*? How can you test your generalizations?

2. Move the cursor over North America on the "Nighttime Lights" map and select. How does changing the scale of the map alter the detail you can see? Is this map a larger or smaller scale than the world map? Describe the distribution of population in the United States. What are the large bright spots? Locate your state on this map and compare it with other parts of the United States. What happens along a line that extends roughly from North Dakota through central Texas? How do you account for this change in the concentration of lights?

3. Move the cursor over the Arabian Peninsula on the "Nighttime Lights" map and select. What is the long vertical thread of light on the left side of the image? Locate Israel. How do you account for the fact that it is different from other areas around it? Locate the Persian Gulf. How do you account for the very intense concentration of light along the western coast of the gulf? Use this map to debate the statement: High concentrations of light correlate to *population density* and level of *economic development*.

4. Move the cursor over Asia on the "Nighttime Lights" map and select. Which part of the map has the greatest concentration of light? How do you account for this? China and India have the largest populations of all the countries of the world. Why are there no areas of high light concentration in either country? Use maps in an atlas to identify the two large areas in the center of the map that have almost no lights. Print a copy of the map. Then make a poster on which you pose and answer questions about Asia based on evidence in this nighttime map.

51. U.S. GEOLOGICAL SURVEY: "SELECTED IMAGE GALLERY"

Site address: http://edcwww.cr.usgs.gov/bin/html_web_store.cgi

Type of data: aerial photographs; satellite images

Key terms: patterns; urban landscapes; oblique; vertical; false color image; time series images

GEOGRAPHIC CONTEXT

Aerial photographs and satellite images invite analysis of *patterns* because of the special perspective that they offer. Patterns in *urban landscapes* become especially evident when viewed from above. For example, the role of transportation lines or natural features in shaping urban growth are often difficult to observe at ground level but assume new meaning from an aerial perspective. Aerial photographs, such as these provided by the U.S. Geological Survey, also allow comparison of patterns at different points in time. Aerial and satellite images enable analysis of relationships between physical and human features, such as human settlements near rivers or potential hazards.

THINKING CRITICALLY

Open the "USGS Selected Image Gallery" site.

1. Select "Cities of the U.S." Scroll down and select the three images of "Washington, D.C." How are the images different? What are some advantages and disadvantages of *oblique* versus *vertical* aerial photographs. Compare the photographs with a large scale map of Washington, D.C. Use the map to help you identify key physical and human features in the photographs. Can you find examples of features in the photograph that the cartographer has selectively omitted from the map? Why might cartographers create a map without all features? Is this a flaw in map-making?

2. Select "NAPP Major Metro of the U.S." Select the photographs of "Dallas, TX" and "Philadelphia, PA." Compare the images in terms of density of land use and transportation lines. In what ways are these two major cities similar or different? How do you account for these similarities and differences? Do further research to evaluate your observations and speculations about these cities. Analyze additional evidence in order to test your conclusions.

3. Select "Cities of the World." Select the *false color image* of "Beijing, China." What do the colors in the image represent? As China continues to industrialize, the competition for different uses of limited land is great. Research the type of agricultural activity conducted in the areas near Beijing. What are some implications if the city continues to expand? Using this image as a focal point, debate rural/agricultural versus urban/industrial use of land in China.

4. Select "Natural Features." Select the *time series images* of "Brazil." What do the colors in these false color images represent? Find out if your county planning or transportation office maintains an archive of aerial photographs of the local area. If available, study time series photographs and make a bulletin board display tracking changes in your local area. Why is it important to note such changes?

52. THE LINCOLN HIGHWAY

Site address: http://www.ugcs.caltech.edu/~jlin/lincoln/

Type of data: maps; narrative; photographs

Key terms: transportation; automobile; highway; cultural landscape; economic growth

GEOGRAPHIC CONTEXT

The development of the United States has been very much influenced by evolving modes of *transportation*. Wagons, steamships, and trains opened the way west, but nothing has had quite the impact of the *automobile*. The automobile allowed personal mobility not previously experienced; the automobile also prompted the spread of *highways* across the landscape. The Lincoln Highway, initiated in 1913, was the first transcontinental highway in the United States.

THINKING CRITICALLY

Open the "Lincoln Highway" site.

1. Select "History." From the sidebar, select the "Historic Newspaper Articles." Read these accounts from 1913 of the opening of the Lincoln Highway. What was public reaction to this event? Study the cartoon in the article from the *San Francisco Examiner*. What is the artist's message? How did the opening of the Lincoln Highway affect life in the United States?

2. Select "Maps and Information by State." On a map of the United States, trace the approximate route of the Lincoln Highway using the information provided at the bottom of the page. Then select one state, perhaps your state or the state nearest to you, perhaps Nebraska. Compare the route of the Lincoln Highway and the routes of present-day interstate highways. Look at the 1924 maps of Nebraska and note the presence of towns along the Lincoln Highway. Are these towns important today? Speculate on the role of major transportation lines in town development. How can you test your hypothesis?

3. Select "Articles." Access the series of articles from the Cedar Rapids, Iowa *Gazette*, "The Lincoln: From Highway to Byway." These articles represent a contemporary look back at an earlier period through markers in the *cultural landscape* (the landscape as altered by human activity). Read the articles and view the route along the highway through the eyes of these reporters. What important clues can you detect in the cultural landscape? What are different people's attitudes toward the highway? Identify an old roadway in your area. Visit it and look at it with new eyes. What clues to the past do you observe? What factors have resulted in the road's being less used today than in the

past? Write a newspaper article describing the road and its place in the history of your area.

4. Locate a list of the interstate highways in your state at (52a) http://www.ihoz.com/ilist.html. Scroll down to "Search the Interstate List by City" and select your state from the drop-down menu, for example North Carolina. Examine the details for each interstate. On a state map, locate the major cities and major intersections with other interstates for each of the highways listed. In what ways is the pattern of interstate highways linked to *economic growth* and development in your state? Why is transportation so important? Find out from the state highway office what highway construction projects are being considered in your state. Speculate on the impact of the completion of a new highway.

53. THE BOSNIAN VIRTUAL FIELDTRIP

Site address: http://geog.gmu.edu/projects/bosnia/default.html

Type of data: maps; photographs; personal accounts

Key terms: political geography; ethnic diversity; virtual field trip; opinion; point of view

GEOGRAPHIC CONTEXT

Political uncertainty marks the landscape of Eastern Europe, particularly in those countries that once made up the former Yugoslavia. Factors that contribute to the ways in which people divide the land are of special concern to *political geographers*. *Ethnic diversity* in the region of Bosnia led to open conflict in this small Balkan country. Cultural icons and the destruction of war mark the landscape and invite study and analysis. Visiting Bosnia to make personal observations is probably impossible but a *virtual field trip*, via the George Mason University Geography Department's special projects, is an option.

THINKING CRITICALLY

On the "GMU Geography Department Research Projects" page, select "The Bosnian Virtual Fieldtrip."

1. Select "Part I. Background." Scroll down and select "Start the Fieldtrip." Follow this self-directed field trip, keeping a travel journal of your responses to the questions posed along the way. Write an essay in response to Question 5 at the end of this part of the fieldtrip.

2. On the "Bosnian Virtual Fieldtrip" main page, select "Part II. People and Places." Again, follow this self-directed fieldtrip and continue your travel journal in response to each question. At the conclusion of Part II, conduct a role

play exercise using the scenarios described in the activity under "Final Analysis."

3. On the "Bosnian Virtual Fieldtrip" main page, select "Part III. Dayton and After." Continue the field trip, again responding to questions posed along the way in your journal. In response to Question 4, put yourself in the place of a Serb who is contemplating relocation. Answer the questions in the form of a dialogue with your brother who has decided not to leave.

4. On the "Bosnian Virtual Fieldtrip" main page, select the discussion topic "Latest news." Scroll down to "Report from Sarajevo" and read this first-hand account of a former journalist and ham radio operator visiting war-torn Sarajevo. Then select and read "Voices from Sarajevo," accounts from citizens of Sarajevo. Compare and contrast the observations and concerns of these people. In what ways were the observations of an outsider similar or different from those of people living in Sarajevo? How do you account for this? Is one position more accurate than the other? Explain.

5. On the "Bosnian Virtual Fieldtrip" main page, select the discussion topic "Should the US be involved in Kosovo?" Read the direct responses of people who have replied to this bulletin board. Analyze the different *opinions* expressed. Why are there so many different *points of view* on issues such as Kosovo or Bosnia? How do you know what is correct? What is your position regarding this difficult issue? Write a set of questions to help you evaluate a situation in which information and opinions seem to be contradictory.

54. THE BALKANS REGIONAL ATLAS

Site address: http://www.odci.gov/cia/publications/balkans/regter.html

Type of data: maps; statistics

Key terms: relationships; spatial phenomena; patterns of change; regional analysis; conflict; boundary; physical environment; regional development

GEOGRAPHIC CONTEXT

Atlases are more than just collections of maps. They offer opportunities to compare and evaluate data; to look for *relationships* between *spatial phenomena*; and to observe *patterns of change* over time. Geographers are especially interested in *regional analysis* as a tool for understanding political tension in particular places. The Balkan region of Europe is one such area that has experienced open conflict and serious disruption of people's lives in recent years. Data collected by the Central Intelligence Agency and presented in this electronic atlas support analysis when travel to the region is impractical.

THINKING CRITICALLY

Open the "Balkan Regional Atlas" main page.

1. Select the map of "Bosnia and Herzegovina." Compare each of the maps of Bosnia and Herzegovina. Use information from each map to develop an essay in which you account for the *conflict* that has plagued these countries in recent years.

2. Select the map of "Croatia" and then the map of "Ethnic Populations." Repeat this step for each of the remaining three countries. Assume the role of Official Cartographer for a United Nations Boundary Commission assigned to the Balkan region. Draft new *boundaries* for the region. Present your map to the class and justify your decisions.

3. Examine the physical map of the region on the "Atlas" main page. Refer also to other physical maps in print atlases. What role do you think the *physical environment* may have played in the lack of stability in this region? Do you think the environment has contributed to the problems experienced by these countries? Test your conclusion by examining surrounding countries. Are there countries with similar physical landscapes? Have they experienced similar conflict? Revisit your conclusion about the role of the environment.

4. Examine the "Minerals & Resources," "Energy," and "Economic Activity" maps for each country. Create a chart in which you compare the countries of the region. Based on available resources, what is the potential for economic development in this region, assuming political stability? Would these countries fare better under some type of economic confederation or with each country acting alone? Conduct additional research on the economic potential of each country. Then carry out a role-play of a conference among the Economic Ministers of the four countries to develop a *regional development* plan.

"The physical environment is modified by human activities largely as a consequence of the ways in which human societies value and use Earth's natural resources, and human activities are also influenced by Earth's physical features and processes" (*Geography for Life* 1994: 35). The relationship between people and the environment is central to the study of geography because:

- human activity has modified Earth to the advantage of some but the disadvantage of others. At the same time human exploitation of Earth's resources has placed the environment at risk.

- prosperity and quality of life are closely linked to people's control and use of Earth's unevenly distributed resources. Consumption patterns are likewise unevenly distributed but control rather than location is the key to resource use.

55. THE GREAT LAKES: AN ENVIRONMENTAL ATLAS AND RESOURCE BOOK

Site address: http://www.cciw.ca/glimr/data/great-lakes-atlas/intro.html

Type of data: maps; photographs; graphics; charts and data sets

Key terms: physical and human properties; land use; pollution; areas of concern

GEOGRAPHIC CONTEXT

Accounting for about 18 percent of the fresh surface water in the world, the Great Lakes of North America are a major resource. They provide fresh water, fish, and transportation, as well as recreation for a large population in the United States and Canada. At the same time, careless use and misuse of the lakes by people have created serious pollution problems, putting these natural treasures at risk. Major industrial centers have developed along the lakeshores. Forestry and agriculture also contribute to the economy. But each of these activities is potentially a source of pollution. *The Great Lakes: An Environmental Atlas and Resource Book* was produced jointly by the government of Canada and the U.S. Environmental Protection Agency. Each section of the atlas can be accessed from the "Table of Contents" main page.

THINKING CRITICALLY

1. From the "Table of Contents," select "Chapter One. Introduction." Read the general description of the Great Lakes region. Then select "Great Lakes Fact-sheet No. 1." Create a graphic profile in which you compare and contrast the *physical and human properties* of the lakes and their connecting waterways. Based on the data in your profile, speculate on which lakes are most likely to be adversely affected by human activity. Justify your conclusions.

2. From the "Table of Contents," select "Chapter Three. People and the Great Lakes—Agriculture." Select the map of "Land Use, Fisheries & Erosion." Describe patterns of *land use*. Scroll down to the section on "Urbanization and Industrial Growth" and select the map of "Employment and Industrial Structure." Study this map to assess patterns of population and industrial activity in the Great Lakes basin. How have people altered the Great Lakes ecosystem? Write a position paper on future limitations on human activity in the Great Lakes region.

3. From the "Table of Contents," select "Chapter Four. The Great Lakes Today." On the opening page of the chapter select the map "Distribution of Population." Describe the patterns you observe. Scroll down to the section on "Control of Pollutants" and select the map "State of the Lakes." Use the map key to analyze the level and types of *pollution* affecting the Great Lakes. Are problems uniformly distributed? Why? Why not? Refer to other maps in the atlas to develop a cause/effect analysis of pollution in the Great Lakes. Present your findings in a poster.

4. From the "Table of Contents," select "Chapter Four. The Great Lakes Today—Geographic Areas of Concern." Read this section to understand what is meant by "Area of Concern." Then select the table "Impaired Uses." Use the key to categories of impairment and the data in the table to map *areas of concern* in the Great Lakes basin. Select and research one site on the map. Then develop a carefully reasoned action plan that takes into account both environmental concerns and human needs. Present and defend your plan to the class.

56. WETMAAP: WETLAND EDUCATION THROUGH MAPS AND AERIAL PHOTOGRAPHY

Site address: http://www.rac.us.edu/wetmaap

Type of data: photographs; aerial photographs; maps; data sets

Key terms: wetlands; human-environment interaction; physical and human characteristics

GEOGRAPHIC CONTEXT

Human activity frequently alters natural environments, often putting them at risk. One such environment is *wetlands* (any land that is periodically waterlogged, either fresh or saline). Throughout the United States people have altered wetlands for recreational use, drained them to create farmland, and filled them in response to growing demand for housing space. At the same time, natural events such as storms and floods have also changed wetlands. Understanding the nature and far-reaching effects of such change is a critical element of the geographic theme of *human-environment interaction*. "WETMAAP," funded by NASA Ames Research Center, provides extensive resources for the study of selected wetlands in the United States, focusing on both physical and human aspects of change.

THINKING CRITICALLY

1. At the bottom of the site main page, select "Sites." Then under "Select a Region" choose "Crescent Lake, Nebraska." Select "Educator Supplement," then scroll down to the sample lesson plan "Finders Keepers!" Follow the suggested procedures to become familiar with the use and interpretation of aerial photographs and topographic maps as sources of information.

2. At the bottom of the site main page, select "Sites." Then under "Select a Region" choose "Mobile Bay, Alabama." Select "Background Slides" to take a photographic tour of the Mobile Bay area. Record your observations of the region in a field journal. Keep two separate columns, distinguishing between *physical and human characteristics* of the place. Select and compare the aerial photographs and maps from 1955–56 and 1988. What changes can be observed? What physical and human interventions might account for these changes? Use additional resources available on this site to extend your analysis.

3. At the bottom of the site main page, select "Sites." Then under "Select a Region" choose "Cape Hatteras." Select "Educator Supplement;" then scroll down to select "Workshop Index." Follow the on-screen prompts to complete the skill and techniques exercises using maps and aerial photographs of the Cape Hatteras area.

4. At the bottom of the site main page, select "Sites." Then select "Complete List of All WETMAAP Study Sites," and "Avery Island." Examine the aerial photographs, satellite image, and topographic and habitat maps available on the site. What kinds of information can be derived from each. What are some advantages and disadvantages of each? Use the time series photographs and maps to identify a pattern of change in the region. Use additional resources to account for the changes observed.

57. WORLD CONSERVATION MONITORING CENTRE

Site address: http://www.wcmc.org.uk

Type of data: maps; statistical data

Key terms: endangered/critically endangered species; forests; scale; marine resources; conservation

GEOGRAPHIC CONTEXT

Sustainable use of Earth's environment and resources depends on accurate knowledge of these resources. The World Conservation Monitoring Centre (WCMC), in collaboration with the United Nations Environment Programme, maintains extensive databases relating to plant, animal, and water resources.

THINKING CRITICALLY

Open the main page of the WCMC site.

1. Select "species" and "species information." Scroll down to select "Species Under Threat." Then select the species listed under "Animals" (or one of the other categories) and review the information provided. Sort the species by general location. Distinguish between species that are *endangered* and those that are *critically endangered*. Create a chart in which you categorize the main reasons that these species are at risk. Select critically endangered species and do additional research to learn about these animals' prospects for survival.

2. Select "forests" and "forest programme." Then select "Forest Information" and the "Generalised World Forest Map." Where are the largest forested areas found? What types of *forests* are in these places? Return to the "Forest Information" page and access "analysis and regional maps." (This is a two-step process.) Select a world region, such as "Russia," and examine the maps and graphs showing forest cover and protection. Compare your observations with data for North America. Return to the "Forest Information" page and select a specific country for closer study, for example, Australia. Select both forest statistics and forest maps and "submit." How does *scale* affect analysis?

3. Select "marine" and "marine programme." From the drop-down country menu, select "Bahamas." What *marine resources* are found in the Bahamas? Note the extent of mangroves and coral reefs. Return to the "Marine Information" page and select the link to the "Coral Reefs and Mangroves of the World" web site. Use this site to learn about the location of coral reefs and mangroves worldwide. What factors put these natural regions at risk? In what ways are these ecosystems valuable to humans?

4. Select "biodiversity assessment." In the side bar select "Biodiversity Profiles and then "ten countries." Select a country for study, for example "Cuba." Select all the data options and "submit." Use the data provided to create a poster highlighting environmental resources and concerns in Cuba. Return to the National Biodiversity Profiles page and select the "Section" drop-down menu. Choose "Investment in *conservation*" and "submit." In the list of countries, select Cuba and several other countries to compare Cuba's investment

in conservation with that in other countries. What factors may affect a country's decisions about investing in conservation?

58. WORLD WILDLIFE FUND GLOBAL NETWORK

Site address: http://panda.org/

Type of data: maps; graphs and charts; photographs; narrative

Key terms: human-environment interaction; relationship; natural systems; climate change; fisheries

GEOGRAPHIC CONTEXT

A central theme of geography has always been the relationship between people and the natural environment. People depend upon the environment to meet their needs; people also impose change upon environmental systems through their actions and exploitation of Earth's resources. Therefore, *human-environment interaction* is pivotal to the study of geography. Many advocacy groups focus on this *relationship* between people and the environment, including the World Wildlife Fund (WWF). Advocacy groups are a valuable source of information but such sources must be approached with a critical eye for possible bias.

THINKING CRITICALLY

Open the "WWF" main page.

1. Select "Living Planet." Then navigate to the "Living Planet Index Report." The "Index Report" provides an online graphic presentation of key indicators selected to measure the planet's health and a downloadable PDF version of the full report. What indicators has WWF selected? Evaluate the usefulness of these indicators as measures of pressure on Earth's *natural systems*. What additional indicators would you choose? Research an additional indicator of your choice and create a poster following the style of the Living Planet Index Report.

2. Select "Climate Change." From the sidebar, select "Climate information" and then "Climate Fact Sheet." Read the fact sheet about *climate change*. Evaluate the document for statements of fact versus opinion. Not everyone agrees with the WWF position on climate change. Research the position that climate change is *not* a threat. Compare the evidence, decide where you stand, and write your own position statement.

3. Select "Endangered Seas," and navigate to "Threatened Fisheries." Read the "Field Story" about fishing in the waters off Mauritania. Identify the various interest groups cited in the article. Is this an isolated issue or does it have significance for people in other places? Refer to the *fisheries* map on this site.

Select one of the threatened areas and research the issues for this place. Then write your own "field story," being sure to address the concerns of all parties involved.

4. Select "Site Map" and navigate to "Country Profiles." Select a country, for example, "Nepal." Review the documents provided. Assume the role of a CNN reporter on special assignment. Script a report on the "State of the Environment—Live from Nepal" and present it to the class. Remember that television reporters have limited time. What are the most important points you need to make? What visual aids do you need to get your message across?

59. GLOBAL TRENDS IN ENVIRONMENT AND DEVELOPMENT

Site address: http://www.wri.org/wri/powerpoints/index.html

Type of data: graphs and charts; maps

Key terms: population; resources; environment; quality of life; consumption patterns

GEOGRAPHIC CONTEXT

In late 1999 the world's *population*, according to United Nations estimates, passed the 6 billion mark. This population is unevenly distributed throughout the world with varying impacts on resources and quality of life. The relationship between people, *resources*, and the *environment* is central to geography. It is also a central focus of World Resources Institute, a non-governmental organization that monitors and collects data on environmental conditions worldwide.

THINKING CRITICALLY

Open the "Global Trends" main page.

1. Scroll to "Population and Human Well-Being." Beginning with the first slide about World Population Growth, work through the slide series, reading each graph or map carefully. Make notes on the main point of each slide. Then use your notes as the basis for an essay discussing the relationship between population growth and *quality of* human *life* at a variety of scales, for example, global, regional, national. How does scale influence the interpretation of trends?

2. Scroll to "Feeding the World." Interpret the slides in this set to address the following questions: How have *consumption patterns* changed over time? How can you account for these changes? Examine the slides in the set, "Production and Consumption." Revisit the questions above and apply the information in these slides to expand upon your answers.

3. Click on the link to "World Resources 1998–99" and follow on-screen prompts to navigate to "Facts and figures" about "Agriculture." Use data from the text and tables on "Sustainable Agriculture" to create a poster presentation that illustrates the linkages among population, food supply, and agriculture.

4. From the Powerpoint index, select "Climate Change." Compare the slide "Atmospheric CO_2 Concentrations" with the World Population Growth slides from the Population and Human Well-Being slide set. Do you think there is a correlation or is this just a coincidence? How can you support your point of view? Collect additional data. Then use presentation software, such as Microsoft PowerPoint, to create a set of slides to make your point. Make a presentation to the class, narrating each slide with information from your research.

60. ENVIRONMENTAL DEFENSE FUND

Site address: http://www.edf.org

Type of data: maps; photographs; graphs; narrative

Key terms: advocacy groups; Amazon rainforest; dams; endangered species; global warming

GEOGRAPHIC CONTEXT

A central theme in the study of geography has always been the relationship between human activity and the natural environment in which we live. In recent years that interest has manifested itself in concerns about the destructive impact of humans, in their ever-increasing numbers, on a fragile environment upon which all depend for life. This concern has led to the emergence of a number of environmental *advocacy groups*, such as the Environmental Defense Fund (EDF). Such organizations are an important source of information about the environment, but because of their advocacy position, information on such sites must be evaluated with care.

THINKING CRITICALLY

Open the "EDF" main page.

1. Navigate to "Search/Index." Under "A," select "Amazon Rainforest." View images of the Amazon rainforest by selecting "Take a Tour." Identify photographs and captions that reflect the advocacy position of the EDF. Now select "See the Burning." Examine the satellite images of fires in the Amazon rainforest. Plot the main locations of burning on a blank map of Brazil and research human activities in these areas that might account for the fires. Form

your own position about human activity and environmental protection in the Amazon rainforest.

2. Navigate to "Search/Index." Under "D," select "Dams." Examine the map "Dams Around the World." Where is the greatest amount of construction taking place? How can you account for this pattern? Select a proposed dam. Research the project and the area to be affected by the construction of the dam. Organize a debate between advocates and opponents of the dam.

3. Navigate to "Search/Index." Under "E," select "Endangered Species." On a world map plot the range of the species identified in the list. Research each species to determine what factors pose the greatest threat to each and what measures are being taken to protect each. Select one species and write a newspaper article with a strong advocacy slant.

4. Navigate to "Search/Index." Under "G," select "Global Warming." Review the resources provided at this site. Develop a set of questions to help you determine the objectivity of the information presented. Does the site present all points of view? Not all experts consider global warming to be a serious problem. How can you gather information to form you own opinion? Search for a site that presents an "anti-global warming" position. Compare the information with that offered by EDF. Make a presentation to the class, presenting evidence from both positions. Then lead a discussion to arrive at consensus.

61. USGS EARTHSHOTS: "SATELLITE IMAGES OF ENVIRONMENTAL CHANGE"

Site address: http://edcwww.cr.usgs.gov/earthshots/slow/tableofcontents
Type of data: satellite images; maps; photographs; narrative
Key terms: satellite image; false-color image

GEOGRAPHIC CONTEXT

Observation of Earth is central to the geographer's craft and satellite images offer a unique perspective from which to view Earth's surface. Patterns and relationships, not visible during ground-level observations, become clear when seen from above. In addition, time-series satellite images reveal patterns of change and encourage analysis of the processes at work, both natural and human. Satellite images from the EROS Data Center of the U.S. Geological Survey, together with maps and background articles, cover a wide range of topics and locations.

THINKING CRITICALLY

1. From the "Earthshots Table of Contents," select "Garden City, Kansas." Follow the on-screen prompts for a tutorial in the reading and interpretation of

satellite images. Use the maps and photographs linked to the site to put the images in perspective. Under "Other help articles," select "Landsat" and then select author Stephen Hall's version of the Landsat story. Read the article and evaluate the author's point of view. Do you agree with the author's position on the role of satellite imagery? Select some images from the "Earthshots" site and make a presentation to the class presenting your point of view.

2. From the "Earthshots Table of Contents," select "Riyadh, Saudi Arabia" under "City" articles. Read the article and follow the onscreen prompts to view the images and maps of Riyadh. Describe the changes that have occurred. Write an essay under the title "When Oil and Water Mix."

3. From the "Earthshots Table of Contents," select "Mount St. Helens, Washington" under "Disaster" articles. Read the article and follow the onscreen prompts to view the images, photographs, and maps of Mount St. Helens. What do the colors in this *"false color" image* represent? Compare the satellite images and the photographs. What are some advantages and disadvantages of each? Do additional research to find out about the human impact of this violent volcanic eruption.

4. The story of the Netherlands' reclamation of land from the sea is well-known. From the "Earthshots Table of Contents," select "Ijsselmeer, Netherlands" under "Water" articles. Read the article and follow the onscreen prompts to view the images, photographs, and maps of the transformation of an arm of the North Sea into productive land. Create a poster presentation in which you illustrate the process of reclamation. Do research to identify other places that have reclaimed land from the sea for human use.

62. CLIMATE PREDICTION CENTER—AFRICAN DESK

Site address: http://www.cpc.ncep.noaa.gov/products/african_desk/index.html

Type of data: maps; charts; narrative

Key terms: climate; drought; climate prediction; country profile; vegetation; food insecurity

GEOGRAPHIC CONTEXT

With much of its population dependent on agriculture, Africa faces a serious challenge in the uncertainty of its *climate*. Unreliable rainfall and periods of extended *drought* threaten the lives and livelihood of many people. *Climate prediction* cannot change climate patterns but it can enable people to plan ahead and prepare for times when normal patterns of rainfall may not occur. The Africa Desk of the National Oceanographic and Atmospheric Administration (NOAA) maintains records of climate patterns in Africa.

THINKING CRITICALLY

Open the main page of the "Climate Prediction Center—African Desk."

1. Select "Monthly Station Data." Examine each of the maps of precipitation and temperature data, but especially the maps of "normal" and "departure from normal" precipitation and temperature. Where in Africa was precipitation above or below normal? Is there any correlation between patterns in departure from normal precipitation and temperature? What is the relationship between temperature and precipitation? How do departures from normal affect people's lives?

2. Select "Seasonal Mean and Anomaly Rainfall Maps." Then select "CPC-Assessment of the 1998 Sahel Rainy Season." Which countries make up the region known as the Sahel? What were rainfall conditions in this region during the period covered by the map? What were rainfall conditions in other parts of West Africa? According to the data provided, which countries experienced lower than normal levels of precipitation? Use the "Country-specific" link at the bottom of the page to create a brief *profile* of each of these countries, for example, population size, mortality rates, percent of labor force in agriculture, and average calorie consumption. Speculate on the impact on people's lives of lower than normal precipitation in these countries? Write a human interest news report about life in the rural area of one of the countries you have investigated.

3. Scroll to the bottom of the page and select "USGS/FEWS Home Page." Then select "Weather Analysis." On the interactive map, select West Africa. Evaluate the condition of *vegetation* compared to previous and average conditions. Scroll down and relate your evaluation of vegetation to rainfall patterns. What generalizations can you make? Test your generalizations by repeating the process of evaluation using the maps for the remaining regions of Africa.

4. Scroll to the bottom of the page and select "USGS/FEWS Home Page." Then select "Bulletins." Scroll down to the "FEWS Special Reports" and select "Current Food Insecurity in Southern Africa, 1998–99." Read the report. Then draft a proposal for a USAID-sponsored food assistance program in the region. Present and defend your proposal to the class. Use maps and data from the report to build a compelling argument in support of the proposal.

Additional sites for food security:

World Food Programme (62a) http://www.wfp.org/index.htm

Global Information and Early Warning System on Food and Agriculture (62b)

http://fao.org/waicent/faoinfo/economic/giews/english/giews.htm

63. SOUTH FLORIDA WATER MANAGEMENT DISTRICT

Site address: http://141.232.1.11/org/bcb/3_bcblinks.html

Type of data: computer enhanced maps

Key terms: landscape; land use; change

GEOGRAPHIC CONTEXT

Computer enhanced maps enable geographers to focus on particular features of the landscape and identify areas of change over time. For example, alteration of the natural environment to accommodate human activities may occur gradually and may lead to problems over the long term. Use of specially enhanced maps, such as these from the South Florida Water Management District, can help geographers trace patterns of change and plan solutions.

THINKING CRITICALLY

From the "South Florida Water Management District" site, select "Interesting Links":

1. Open "Map of the District in 1900." Use the map key to identify *landscape* features in south Florida in 1900. Note in particular the area of sawgrass. Research the population and economy of south Florida around the turn of the century. Create maps and charts that show the human-environment relationship at that point in time.

2. Open "Map of the District in 1953." Compare this map with that of south Florida in 1900. Which parts of the state experienced the greatest *change*. Use a transparency to make an overlay of the region, marking those areas of significant change. Identify the counties involved and research population and economic changes that occurred since 1900. How is population change reflected in this map even though population is not in the map key?

3. Open "Map of the District in 1973." Compare this map with those of south Florida in 1900 and 1953. In particular, note the areas of purple, red, and orange. Speculate on some consequences of the human alteration of south Florida's natural environment, as shown in the maps from 1900, 1953, and 1973. Use additional links on this site to research this topic. Research changes in south Florida's population since 1973. Based on patterns in these maps and current population patterns, what do you think a current *landscape/land use* map of the area would show? How can you test your hypothesis?

4. Research landscape/land use change in your state or in the region of the state in which you live. What sources of information might you use? Visit the local library or historical society to locate images from an earlier time. Collect data from various state or county agencies. Use blank maps of the state to create

a series of maps, modeled after the south Florida maps, showing the changes in the natural environment and in the human use of the land.

64. EVERGLADES NATIONAL PARK

Site address: http://www.nps.gov/ever/presskit/index.htm

Type of data: maps; statistics; narrative

Key terms: public education; interest groups; regional planning; point of view; legislation

GEOGRAPHIC CONTEXT

Everglades National Park in South Florida is one of many areas managed by the U.S. National Park Service. The Park Service not only protects and preserves this important natural area; it also provides information and *public education* opportunities about the park. As a part of its information outreach, the Park Service provides an online "Press Kit" which includes a variety of information about physical properties of the park, issues facing the region, and different people's perspectives on the park's importance.

THINKING CRITICALLY

1. From the "Press Kit," select "Area Statistics." Use information from this page to create an illustrated poster that profiles Everglades National Park. Locate a map of the park and label significant points of interest. Convert the "Chart of Annual Visitation" into a graph. Evaluate the overall trend in visitation. Note irregularities in the trend. Research periods of unusual drops in visitation and try to account for these periods of decline.

2. From the "Press Kit," select "Issues." Identify the major issues facing Everglades National Park. What *interest groups* are involved in these issues? Research the issues. Then convene a mock *regional planning* conference to debate the issues facing the Park. How can the interests of various groups (farmers, ranchers, businesses, homeowners, etc.) be met without jeopardizing the Park and its unique plants and animals?

3. From the "Press Kit," select "Quotes." Read these quotes from various supporters of Everglades National Park. Analyze the quotes to identify the speaker's *point of view*. Are the statistics cited accurate? Is there bias? Have the quotes been taken out of context? How can you tell? Can an alternative position be developed? Select one or more of the quotes and research the author's position further in order to evaluate the National Park Service's objectivity in choosing the quote for this site.

4. From the "Press Kit," select "Management Objectives." Scroll to the bottom of the page and select "Legislative Direction." Read these abstracts from the 1934

Everglades Establishment Act and the 1989 Everglades National Park Protection and Expansion Act. Is present *legislation* sufficient to meet the Park's current management objectives? Draft two proposals for additional legislation, one from the perspective of the National Park Service and another from the perspective of Florida developers. Then debate the issues.

65. SPACE RADAR IMAGES OF EARTH

Site address: http://www.jpl.nasa.gov/radar/sircxsar

Type of data: remotely sensed images

Key terms: physical and human features; regional development

GEOGRAPHIC CONTEXT

Remotely sensed images, such as these from the National Aeronautics and Space Administration (NASA), provide geographers and other scientists with a special perspective on Earth's surface. Radar has the distinct advantage of being able to collect information under conditions that would preclude the use of other types of image recorders. Imaging radar is able to "see" through cloud cover, does not require sunlight, and can even penetrate vegetation and ice under certain circumstances. Imaging radar is yet another tool that geographers use to record and analyze changes on Earth's surface.

THINKING CRITICALLY

1. Select "Image Category: Cities." Select several cities, for example, Boston, Massachusetts; Houston, Texas; Salt Lake City, Utah; and San Diego, California. Examine the images of these cities and record your observations about the physical properties of each. Are they compact or sprawling? In what ways do *physical features* seem to have influenced the development of each city? What *human features* are visible? What features appear to be common to all the cities? Are any unique? Try to locate an aerial view of a city in your state for comparison.

2. On a map of Brazil, locate the area of Bebedouro (9°S, 40.2°W). Based on your analysis of the map, describe the physical and human characteristics of this area. Now, from NASA's "Space Radar Images of Earth" site, select "Image Category: Ecology and Agriculture," and the image "Bebedouro, Brazil." What characteristics are visible in the radar image that were not included in the map? How can such images aid in *regional development* projects?

3. "Select Image Category: Rivers." Select "Rhine River, France, Germany." Use the key to colors provided in the narrative passage with the image to analyze the human use of this major European river valley. Research population and

economic information about the Rhine Valley and use the image to make an oral presentation about this major industrial region.

4. "Select Image Category: Volcanoes." Select images of the shield volcanoes "Kilauea" and "Mauna Loa," both in Hawaii. Compare these with images of conic volcanoes such as those found in "Kamchatka, Russia," "Central Java, Indonesia," and "Mt. Ranier, Washington State." Based on your observations, what generalizations can you make about the physical characteristics of shield and conic volcanoes? How can you test your conclusions? Do further research to create a set of criteria for distinguishing between these two types of volcanoes. Present your findings in an illustrated poster that includes facts, figures, maps, and images.

66. MISSISSIPPI RIVER BASIN

Site address: http://www.epa.gov/msbasin/

Type of data: maps, graphs; charts; statistical data

Key terms: watershed; water quality; contamination

GEOGRAPHIC CONTEXT

Draining most of the interior of the country, the Mississippi River Basin is the largest and one of the most important *watersheds* (drainage area of a river or river system) in the United States. People depend on the river for drinking water, irrigation water, transportation, recreation, energy, waste disposal, and numerous other functions. With so many uses and users associated with the river, the health of the river is a critical issue. The Office of Water of the U.S. Environmental Protection Agency monitors the country's rivers and *water quality*.

THINKING CRITICALLY

Open the "Mississippi River Basin" main page.

1. Select "The Basin and Its Watersheds." Note that the main basin includes seven sub-basins. Select one sub-basin, for example, "Lower Mississippi." Which states are included in this sub-basin? Select "Watershed Health of this area" to get an overview of water quality issues. Note the extent of "more serious" water quality problems. Return to the main basin map and select another sub-basin. Repeat your analysis of "more serious" water quality problems and continue until you have a profile of the entire river basin. Does water quality vary within the basin? Can you observe patterns in the occurrence of poor water quality? Speculate on possible associations between human activity and areas of "more serious" water quality problems.

2. Select "Issues." Read the paragraph about "Hypoxia." What is this problem?

Is it unique to the Mississippi River Basin? Scroll down and select the link to the U.S. Geological Survey document "Contamination in Mississippi River." What other *contamination* issues does the basin face? Read the Executive Summary to establish general knowledge. Then prepare a presentation addressing issues facing the basin and its inhabitants.

3. Select "The Basin and Its Watersheds." Then select the "Ohio" sub-basin and within that sub-basin, the state of "Pennsylvania." Select the city of "Pittsburgh." Pittsburgh lies in the center of a region once known for coal mining and steel manufacturing. Pose a hypothesis about the impact of these activities on water quality in the Pittsburgh area. Now use information from the "Environmental Profile" to test your hypothesis.

4. Select "EPA Activities." Then select "EPA Testimony." Read this document which was presented to the Senate Subcommittee on Oceans and Fisheries in 1998. Assume the role of a Senator serving on this subcommittee and draft a response to this testimony. What action do you support? Then research current Senate actions pending on issues raised.

Additional watershed sites:

Activities in the Chesapeake Bay Region (U.S. Geological Survey) (66a)

http://mapping.usgs.gov/mac/chesbay/index.html

The Chesapeake Bay Program (66b)

http://www.chesapeakebay.net/

67. RIVERS IN PERIL

Site address: http://irn.org/programs.html

Type of data: narrative

Key terms: river; advocacy; bias; cost-benefit analysis; objectivity; point of view

GEOGRAPHIC CONTEXT

Throughout history *rivers* have been focal points of human settlement but as such they have also been unintentional targets of abuse and misuse. Rivers are a source of water for both home and industry, a means of transportation, and a place to dump our waste. The International Rivers Network (IRN) is an environmental *advocacy* organization that provides extensive information on selected rivers around the world and campaigns against projects that have negative impacts on river systems.

THINKING CRITICALLY

1. From the drop-down menu, select "Three Gorges." This is the site of China's controversial dam project on the Yangtze (Chang) River. Read the "Background," including the critical essay by Chinese journalist Shui Fu, "A Profile of Dams in China." What arguments does this excerpt put forward? Identify statements that appear to reflect the *bias* of the source. How can you evaluate the other side of the argument? Select articles from the "Press Advisories" and the "Articles and Updates." Evaluate these articles for objectivity. Create a chart in which you present arguments both for and against the Three Gorges Dam.

2. From the drop-down menu, select "Narmada." The focus of the selection is the Narmada River in western India. Research life in the Narmada River Valley. How many people would be affected by this complex dam and irrigation project? Are all effects negative? Review the press releases and articles on the "IRN" site. Then draft a counter-argument in defense of the project. Present both sides to the class and hold a vote for or against construction of the dam.

3. From the drop-down menu, select "Lesotho." Use suggested links to research the "Lesotho Highlands Water Project" in Lesotho and neighboring South Africa. What is the proposed purpose of this project? Create a chart that analyzes the *costs* and the *benefits* of this project, taking into account both short- and long-term considerations. Write a script for a role-play in which various people affected by the project are being interviewed by you, a visiting foreign journalist.

4. From the "Rivers in Peril" site, navigate to the "IRN" home page. Select "About Rivers and Dams," then read the articles under "What Do River Development Projects Do?" Evaluate these articles for *objectivity*. Develop a set of questions to guide the use of information available from an advocacy group. Should you avoid advocacy sources? Can you gain useful information from a source, even if it promotes a particular *point of view*? Identify examples from these articles to support your position.

68. WHERE DOES MY DRINKING WATER COME FROM?

Site address: http://www.epa.gov/surf2/surf98/wimdw.html

Type of data: maps; statistical data; graphs

Key terms: resource management; source; watershed; water quality; impairment; public health

GEOGRAPHIC CONTEXT

Water is one of the basic requirements for life, but we often take its availability for granted. *Resource management* and conservation is a central concern to geographers because it represents the close connection between people and the natural environment. The first step toward protecting water resources is knowing where they originate and the path they take from *source* to kitchen faucet. In the United States monitoring the quality of water resources is the responsibility of the Environmental Protection Agency.

THINKING CRITICALLY

1. To answer the question, Where does my drinking water come from? enter the name of the county in which you live and submit, for example "Cleveland." The search function will list all the Cleveland counties in the United States and you must select the one you want, in this example, "Cleveland County, North Carolina." Locate your community in the chart and note the name of the *watershed* (drainage area of a river or river system) that supplies your water, in this example "Upper Broad." Select the watershed to view a map. In the list of counties select your county again to learn what other watersheds may be in the county. Locate the watershed on a map of the county.

2. Locate the site page for your watershed (see #1, above). Select the "Index of Watershed Indicators" under "Environmental Profile" to evaluate *water quality* in your county. Interpret the graphs that indicate the health of the watershed and research possible causes of any water problems that exist in your county. Water quality is of concern to all citizens of the county. Present your findings in the form of a newspaper article.

3. Locate the site page for your watershed (see #1, above). Select "1998 Impaired Water" under "Environmental Profile." Analyze the map of the watershed to locate areas of *impairment*. Use information from the accompanying table to identify potential sources of impairment. Select one or two sites near you and plan a visit to the site. Gather your own information about water quality, potential impairment, and plans to correct the problem. Organize your findings in a set of maps, graphs, and charts that you can share with the class.

4. Locate the site page for your watershed (see #1, above). Under "Environmental Profile," access information about facilities regulated by the EPA. Create a map using different symbols for toxic releases, hazardous wastes, and superfund sites. What patterns are revealed? Are these regulated facilities clustered or dispersed? What *public health* issues are raised by the locations of these facilities? Research laws and regulations in your county governing water pollution.

69. INDEX OF WATERSHED INDICATORS

Site address: http://www.epa.gov/surf2/iwi/

Type of data: maps; charts; statistical data

Key terms: water resource; indicator; watershed; population distribution; economic activity; water quality

GEOGRAPHIC CONTEXT

Water has been described as our most precious resource. Without it, life as we know it is not possible. The United States as a country has abundant water resources but they are not evenly distributed; and as population increases, the demand for water becomes ever greater. In addition the pressures of population, agricultural and industrial activity, and use of technology often put water resources at risk. The Index of Watershed Indicators (IWI), compiled by the Environmental Protection Agency, monitors the quality of all water resources in the United States, including rivers, wetlands, and coastal waters.

THINKING CRITICALLY

1. On the "IWI" main page, select "Understanding the IWI." Then select "Introduction to the Index of Watershed Indicators" and the "Indicators Report." Open the Environmental Indicators document (in either PDF or HTML format) and navigate to "II. Water Resources." Use information from this document to create an illustrated profile of *water resources* in the United States. Refer to "Fact Sheets on Indicators" for additional information.

2. On the IWI main page, select "IWI National Maps, Factsheets & Data." Identify the *indicators* used in the index. What is the rationale for each indicator? For each indicator, access the national map and identify problem areas for the indicator. Note, in particular, the status of the area in which you live. Select an indicator that shows problems in your state and access the detailed data that is the basis of the national map. What is the suspected source of the problem? What actions are being taken to address the problem?

3. On the "IWI" main page, select "IWI National Maps, Factsheets & Data." Under regional maps, identify the *watershed* region (drainage area of a river or river system) in which your state is located, for example, Utah is in Region 8. Note the occurrence and location of "More Serious Water Quality Problems." Now work through each of the indicators, examining the status of your region for each. Which indicators pose particular problems for your region? Where are the problem areas? Compare your findings with maps showing *population distribution* and *economic activities* in the region. Are there any correlations that suggest connections? Create a set of map overlays to make your point.

4. On the "IWI" main page, select "Locate Your Watershed." Follow the onscreen instructions to locate your town or county, for example, "Mecklenburg County" in North Carolina. Scroll down and access the "Environmental Profile." Continue to follow onscreen instructions to access the profile for the county you are seeking. Use the graphs and supporting data tables to prepare

a report on *water quality* in your county. What are the problem areas? Interview the local water commissioner to determine what plans are in place to ensure the quality of the county's water supply.

70. STATE OF THE LAND

Site address: http://www.nhq.nrcs.usda.gov/land/home.html

Type of data: maps

Key terms: land use; generalization; scale; erosion; location; water problems; freshwater consumption

GEOGRAPHIC CONTEXT

Although employing a very small percent of the labor force, agriculture remains an important part of the U.S. economy. The continuing productivity of agriculture depends in part of the condition of the land. The U.S. Department of Agriculture maintains a national inventory of land use and conservation practices on rural land.

THINKING CRITICALLY

From the "State of the Land" main page sidebar, select "Maps, Facts, & Figures." Then select "Maps of the state of the Land."

1. From the Index of maps, select "Geography of Hope." Under Maps, select "Dominant Land Uses, 1992." Describe the patterns visible on the map. What are the categories of *land use*? Which categories account for the largest land areas? Locate your state on the map? Do you agree with the *generalization* applied to your state? What are some problems inherent in generalizing information at the national level? Locate a map of land use for your state and compare it with the national map. How does *scale* affect the presentation of data?

2. From the Index of maps, select "Soil Erosion." Under Maps, select "Change in Average Annual Soil Erosion by Wind and Water on Cropland and CPR Land, 1982–1992." Where has *erosion* increased? Where has it decreased? What is happening in your state? Contact the state agriculture office to find out what measures are being taken to deal with problems of soil erosion. Refer to other maps in the soil erosion index and write a newspaper article about soil erosion in your state.

3. From the Index of maps, select "Agricultural Productivity." Under Maps, select "Patterns of Agricultural Diversity." Examine the patterns visible on the map and consider the question: Why are certain economic activities located where they are? How is *location* influenced by physical conditions of the environment? How is it influenced by human factors such as proximity to pop-

ulation centers/markets? What role does technology play in the location of particular agricultural activities?

4. From the Index of maps, select "Water Supply." Under Maps, select "Freshwater Consumption as a Percentage of Local Average Precipitation." What generalizations can you make about the potential for *water problems* in the United States? What role does agriculture play in areas where consumption exceeds average annual precipitation? Locate additional maps from the "Index of Maps" to help you answer this question. What other sources of demand might contribute to these high consumption levels? What additional information will you need to answer this question? Gather additional information. Then lead a discussion of the following questions: What are the sources of demand in areas where *freshwater consumption* is greater than annual average precipitation? What sources of water other than precipitation are there? What problems are likely to arise as a result of non-sustainable use of water?

71. BPAMOCO STATISTICAL REVIEW OF WORLD ENERGY, 1999

Site address: http://www.bpamoco.com/_nav/energy/index.htm

Type of data: statistical data sets; maps; graphs

Key terms: energy resources; fossil fuels; alternative energy

GEOGRAPHIC CONTEXT

The spread of industrialization and technology worldwide has been paralleled by an ever-increasing demand for *energy resources*. Countries that possess or have access to energy resources, especially *fossil fuels*, have enjoyed a particular advantage in the global economy. However, concerns about environmental safety and dwindling supplies of petroleum have directed attention to *alternative energy* sources. The Statistical Review of World Energy, published annually by British Petroleum (now merged with Amoco) provides access to extensive, long-term data on most major energy sources.

THINKING CRITICALLY

On the "World Energy" main page, select "BPAmoco Statistical Review of World Energy 1999."

1. From the sidebar menu, select "1998 in Review." Read this narrative passage, extracting important statistical indicators. Use this data to construct a graphic profile of energy production and consumption for the year. Analyze the patterns. What correlation appears to exist between energy consumption and

other measures of economic well-being? How can you test any apparent correlation?

2. From the sidebar menu, select "Oil." Scroll down and select "Trade Movements" under "Other information in this section." Examine the world map and make observations about patterns in oil trade. Then select "Trade movements" (this requires access to MS Excel 5.0) to view data for major participants in oil trade over the past decade. Which countries or regions are the major oil traders? What share of world imports and exports does the United States control? Graph the long-term import and export data for major traders. What trends can be observed? How do you account for these trends? In what ways may these trends have affected people's lives in your community? Based on past trends, speculate on trends for the next five years.

3. From the sidebar menu, select "Oil" and then "Reserves." Identify the countries or regions that control the major oil reserves. Repeat this step for "Natural Gas" and "Coal." Given the importance of energy resources in today's world, speculate on the political and economic significance of the distribution of these major energy reserves. Write an editorial article in which you present your viewpoint on "Energy in the World of Today and Tomorrow."

4. From the sidebar menu, select "Nuclear energy." Interpret the graph in order to describe the use of nuclear energy worldwide. Scroll down and open the Excel workbook to view data for this section. Compare data for use of nuclear and hydroelectric energy. What trends can be observed? Which regions are major users of these non-fossil fuel energy sources? Do further research in order to form an opinion on the advantages and disadvantages of various types of energy.

USES OF GEOGRAPHY

"Knowledge of geography enables people to develop an understanding of the relationships between people, places, and environments over time—that is, of Earth as it was, is, and might be" (*Geography for Life* 1994: 35).

- Geography is the spatial stage on which temporal events are played out. Everything occurs somewhere. Human actions are shaped by their perceptions of the world around them.

- Keys to the past are embedded in the landscapes of today. Physical features, as well as human imprints on the landscape, offer a window on events that have occurred before.

- Just as knowledge of geography allows us to look back with new understanding, so does it equip us to anticipate and plan for events still to come. Geographic skills of observation and analysis provide the foundation for informed decision-making.

72. LIFE IN HAWAII

Site address: http://www.soest.hawaii.edu/GG/HCV/COAN/coan-intro.html

Type of data: first-person account

Key terms: perception; observation; bias; volcanic activity

GEOGRAPHIC CONTEXT

People's *perceptions* of the environment influence the ways in which they live and use available resources. However, people's perceptions change over time. Geographers often rely on autobiographical accounts and travel journals to understand the point of view of people in earlier periods of time. Such writings provide a window on familiar places at a different point in time. This helps us to understand how and why people lived as they did; it also affords us new perspectives on places today. One such account is Titus Coan's "Life in Hawaii," first published in 1882.

THINKING CRITICALLY

Open the main page of "Life in Hawaii" and navigate to the Table of Contents.

1. Select Chapter II and read Coan's account of his journey to Hawaii. Trace the journey on a map, noting places and dates mentioned in the account. Make a list of problems encountered by Coan and his fellow travelers during the journey. Compare Coans' experiences to those likely to be encountered by someone traveling to Hawaii today. Coan's destination was Hilo, on the island of Hawaii. How did he describe Hilo? What is Hilo like today?

2. Select Chapters XIII and XIV and read Coan's account of his visits to the Marquesas Islands in 1860 and 1867. Locate the Marquesas Islands on a map of the Pacific Basin. As you read these chapters, evaluate Coan's skills of *observation*? What types of things did he notice? Do you feel confident about his descriptions of places he visited? Why? Identify examples from the book to support your opinion. Search for pictures of the Marquesas Islands today and compare them with Coan's verbal images.

3. Select Chapter XVII and read Coan's account of the Hawaiian people. What was the reason for Coan's journey to Hawaii? How is this reflected in his description of the Hawaiian people? Print a copy of this chapter and highlight those words or phrases that reflect Coan's *biases*. Do people today have similar biases about people in distant places? Select a distant place currently in the news and prepare a short questionnaire about the people living there. Administer the questionnaire to a diverse group and evaluate the results. What have you learned from this exercise?

4. Chapters XVIII through XXIII are an account of *volcanic activity* on the island of Hawaii during Coan's stay there. In particular, read Chapter XXII which records the 1868 eruption of Kilauea volcano. Outline the physical consequences of the eruption that Coan described. Use the link at the end of the chapter to access the "Hawaii Center for Volcanology" home page and navigate to the site for Kilauea volcano. This volcano remains active more than one hundred years after Titus Coan experienced its fury. Read the accounts and looks at the photographs on this site and compare the current activity with that described by Coan. Assume the voice of Titus Coan and write an epilogue to his 1882 book describing current activity at Kilauea.

73. THE GREAT 1906 EARTHQUAKE AND FIRE

Site address: http://www.sfmuseum.org/1906/06.html

Type of data: maps and charts; newspaper articles; first-person accounts

Key terms: earthquake

GEOGRAPHIC CONTEXT

Earthquakes are one of the major natural hazards that disrupt people's lives. The United States has a lengthy history of destructive earthquakes ranging from Charleston, South Carolina to New Madrid, Missouri to San Francisco, California. Despite the risks associated with these unpredictable natural events, people continue to live in areas prone to earthquake activity. Records from the 1906 San Francisco earthquake, archived by the Museum of the City of San Francisco, allow us to step back in time and observe the destruction and evaluate people's response at a time when much less was known about these powerful Earth events.

THINKING CRITICALLY

1. Scroll to the bottom of the "1906 Earthquake" page and select "Gladys Hansen's Earthquake Almanac 1769–1994." On a large map of California plot the location of the *earthquakes* felt in the state during this 200+ year period. Develop a system of colors and symbols so that you can differentiate time periods and intensity. What pattern do you observe? Are some areas more prone to earthquakes than others? Is there any correlation between frequency and intensity? Based on what you have learned, speculate on areas most likely to be affected by future earthquakes.

2. On the "1906 Earthquake" page, select "April 18–23 Earthquake Timeline." Read this summary of events. Then locate news stories describing a recent major earthquake in California, such as the one that occurred in Northridge. Compare the accounts of damage and injury. What are some similarities and differences? Are people better prepared today to deal with the effects of an earthquake than in 1906? Support your opinion with specific examples.

3. On the "1906 Earthquake" page, select "Earthquake Newspaper Clippings." Scroll down to the section on "Relief and Recovery" and select the article "Lessons Learned from the Charleston Earthquake." Read this account of the 1886 Charleston earthquake. Also access the photographs from Charleston that are linked to the site. Return to the main page and select "Eyewitness Accounts" and then "Memories of the Earthquake." Compare these two accounts of destructive earthquakes. Both authors were young boys at the time of the earthquakes. How might age have affected their perspective? Compare their accounts of events. In what ways were their experiences similar or different? Read additional accounts of each earthquake in order to evaluate the accuracy of these articles.

4. Earthquake damage was not uniform throughout the San Francisco area. On the "1906 Earthquake" page, select "Earthquake Newspaper Clippings." Scroll down to "Earthquake and Fire Damage" and scan the articles listed. On a street map of the San Francisco area plot information gathered from the articles to determine patterns of damage. Research further to learn about the role of geology and landfills in the pattern of destruction in San Francisco.

Additional historical earthquake sites:

"The 1886 Charleston, South Carolina Earthquake" (73a)

http://www.eas.slu.edu/Earthquake_Center/1886EQ/index.html

"The Virtual Times: The Great New Madrid Earthquake" (1811–1812) (73b)
http://www.hsv.com/genlintr/newmadrd/index.htm

74. INFLUENZA 1918

Site address: http://www.hsv.com/genlintr/newmadrd/index.htm
Type of data: narrative; map
Key terms: spatial dimension; epidemic; pattern; diffusion

GEOGRAPHIC CONTEXT

Because of its *spatial dimensions* (areal extent), geographers are interested in the spread of diseases. Few *epidemics* have affected the United States population so dramatically as the influenza epidemic of 1918. This online site for the Public Broadcasting System encourages consideration of the mechanisms and impact of epidemic disease on a population.

THINKING CRITICALLY

1. On the "Influenza 1918" main page select "The Film and More" to read a "Transcript" of the television program. How does the first person voice of this transcript influence your response to the message? Now select the interviews with experts in the field. What factors contributed to the spread of this epidemic throughout the country? What was the impact?

2. On the "Influenza 1918" main page select "Special Feature." Read the "Letter from Camp Devens, MA," written by a doctor trying to deal with the impact of the disease. Scroll down and read the interview with Dr. Taubenberger about the prospects for future epidemics. Identify the main points that Dr. Taubenberger makes and create a public information brochure about the risk of another influenza outbreak in the United States.

3. On the "Influenza 1918" main page select "Timeline" and "Maps." On a map of the United States plot the events and places identified in the timeline of the 1918 Influenza epidemic. What *patterns* do you observe? Describe the spread of this disease. Compare your map with the animated map on the site. Where did the disease begin? How did it spread? What type of *diffusion* is demonstrated by this pattern of spread? Note which areas were the last to be affected? How can you account for this?

4. Research other diseases, past and present, that have assumed epidemic proportions. Begin by going to the main site of the national Centers for Disease Control ([74a] http://www.cdc.gov). Gather information about several diseases that affect the population of the United States. Locate areas most affected on a map. Identify the symptoms, ways in which the diseases are spread, and measures to control the spread of the diseases. Construct posters that inform others of the risk of epidemic disease.

75. PERRY-CASTAÑEDA LIBRARY MAP COLLECTION

Site address: http://www.lib.utexas.edu/Libs/PCL/Map_collection/Map_collection.html

Type of data: maps

Key terms: conflict and cooperation; ethnic violence; territorial claim

GEOGRAPHIC CONTEXT

In the closing years of the twentieth century some world regions have been plagued with instability ranging from tension to civil unrest to open conflict. Terms such as "ethnic cleansing" and "religious fundamentalism" appear frequently in news accounts. Geographers are concerned with patterns of conflict because of their impact on the spatial organization of Earth. Conflict may result in changes in boundaries or in the movement of large groups of people. One way to understand current conflicts or anticipate those possible in the future is to study human patterns on maps. The Perry-Castañeda Library Map Collection at the University of Texas is one source of such maps.

THINKING CRITICALLY

1. On the "Map Collection" main page, select "Maps of Europe." Then navigate to "Yugoslavia, Former—Maps." Scroll down to "The Region and Former Yugoslavia Maps" and select "Former Yugoslavia—Ethnic Majorities 1992." Analyze the patterns visible in the map. Refer to other maps of the region of the former Yugoslavia, as well. Based on evidence from the maps, write an essay explaining why this region was plagued by conflict throughout much of the decade of the 1990s. Speculate on the future of this region.

2. On the "Map Collection" main page, select "Maps of Asia." Scroll down and select "Central Asia (Major Ethnic Groups) 1993." Examine this map carefully. Research the countries of this region. Then make a chart in which you compare factors for potential *conflict and cooperation* in this region. Lead a class discussion about the future of this region. What factors contribute to instability? What are some unifying factors? Form an opinion about the future of the region based on the evidence collected.

3. On the "Map Collection" main page, select "Maps of Asia." Scroll down and select "Sri Lanka Maps." Under Thematic Maps, select "Sri Lanka." Examine the maps of ethnic communities and religions, population density, and land use and economic activity. Search the files of a major newspaper (for example, *The Washington Post* at [18a] http://www.washingtonpost.com) for articles about *ethnic violence* in Sri Lanka. Read the articles and study the maps. Assume the role of advisor to the U.S. Secretary of State. Write a position paper recommending U.S. policy regarding Sri Lanka.

4. On the "Map Collection" main page, select "Maps of Polar Regions and Oceans." Examine each of the maps listed for the "Antarctic Region." Note the locations of research stations and *territorial claims*. Human activity in Antarctica has been limited to research by the terms of the Antarctic Treaty. Investigate the terms of the treaty and the claims made by various countries. Convene a mock "Conference on the Future of Antarctica" and debate the existing claims and future use of this frozen outpost. For example, should resources under the ice be exploited? Should increasing numbers of tourists be allowed to visit? Should parts of Antarctica be set aside as wildlife preserves? Which countries have a right to territory in Antarctica?

Additional sovereignty site:

"Aloha! Hawai'i Independent & Sovereign"—an example of an independence movement within the United States (75a)

http://hawaii-nation.org/index.html

The Internet abounds with aids to teaching. Samples of the types of primary sources of interest to geographers have been provided in the preceding sections. There are also many general geography megasites with links to both primary and secondary sources that complement units found in typical geography courses. Other sites provide links to large collections of online maps. In addition, there are sites that offer guidelines for using primary sources in the curriculum and for evaluating and selecting quality sites on the Internet.

Geography Megasites

1. "GEOSOURCE" (Utrecht University, Netherlands) http://www.library.uu.nl/geosource/index.html. Extensive list of links, categorized by major topical domains of geography.

2. "WCSU List: Geography Internet Resources" (Western Connecticut State University) http://www.wcsu.ctstateu.edu/socialsci/geores.html. Links to general sites, mapping sites, and topical sites of interest to geographers.

3. "World Wide Web Resources" (Texas A&M University) http://worldroom.tamu.edu/WWWRes.htm. Wide-ranging site with links to topical and regional information, organizations, news and currents events, and instructional aids.

4. "Internet Resources for Geography and Geology" (University of Wisconsin—Stevens Point) http://www.uwsp.edu/acaddept/geog/resour.htm. Multilayered site with extensive links organized by major topics of geography.

5. "Geography Hotlist" (Franklin Institute Science Museum) http://sln.fi.edu/tfi/hotlists/geography.html. More than fifty links to a wide variety of geography-related sites.

6. "Statistical Resources on the Web" (University of Michigan) http://www.lib.umich.edu/libhome/Documents.center/stats.html. Links to statistical data bases ranging from agriculture to weather.

7. "Geography Netlinks" (About.com) http://geography.about.com/. Index of interesting sites, of varying quality and source, related to geography, organized alphabetically and by topic.

8. "The CTI Geo-Information Gateway" (University of Leicester, UK) http://www.geog.le.ac.uk/cti/info.html. On-line index to organizations and research centers, data libraries, educational material, and electronic journals related to geography and arranged by thematic topics.

Map Collections

1. "Oddens's Bookmarks" (Utrecht University, Netherlands) http://oddens.geog.uu.nl/index.html. Links to map collections worldwide; over 6000 links; organized by type and category; special section listing new additions to list.

2. "Maps and References" (University of Iowa) http://www.cgrer.uiowa.edu/servers/servers_references.html. Extensive collection of online map sites organized by regions; special section on interactive maps.

3. "Perry-Castañeda Library Map Collection" (University of Texas) http://www.lib.utexas.edu/Libs/PCL/Map_collection/Map_collection.html. Large collection of maps organized by major regions.

4. "Bodleian Library Map Room" (Oxford University, UK) http://www.bodley.ox.ac.uk/nnj/ Annotated list of links to maps and map collections worldwide; includes many historical maps.

5. "Geography and Map Division" (Library of Congress) http://memory.loc.gov/ammem/gmdhtml/gnrlhome.html. An extensive, searchable collection of historical and contemporary maps covering such diverse categories as "Cities and Towns," "Discovery and Exploration," and "Places in the News."

6. "North America Map Archive" (University of Oregon) http://darkwing.uoregon.edu/~atlas/america/maps.html. Historical and cultural maps of the United States covering such topics as territorial expansion and slavery; some interactive maps.

Critical Thinking

1. "Critical Thinking Across the Curriculum" http://www.kcmetro.cc.mo.us/longview/ctac/ctac.htm Concrete suggestions for integrating critical thinking into all classes.

2. Center for Critical Thinking (Sonoma State University) http://www.criticalthinking.org/ An entire site devoted to the theory and practice of critical thinking; separate links for college/university and primary/secondary education.

Using Primary Sources

"Using Primary Sources in the Classroom" (Library of Congress) http://memory.loc.gov/ammem/ndlpedu/primary.html. Although specifically designed for use in history classes, easily adapted to geography classes.

Locating Internet Sites

"Finding Information on the Internet: A Tutorial" http://www.lib.berkeley.edu/TeachingLib/Guides/Internet/FindInfo.html. Step-by-step guidelines, ranging from start-up basics to advanced search strategies.

Evaluating Internet Sites

1. "Evaluating Web Sites: Criteria and Tools" http://www.library.cornell.edu/okuref/research/webeval.html. Criteria for site evaluation; links to other evaluation sites.

2. "Evaluating Web Resources" http://www2.widener.edu/Wolfgram-Memor-

ial-Library/webeval.htm. Checklists and a module for teaching how to evaluate the content of Internet sites; includes sample web pages.

3. "Thinking Critically about World Wide Web Resources" http://www.library.ucla.edu/libraries/college/instruct/web/critical.htm. Question-based guidelines for evaluating information on the Internet; link to companion site for "Thinking Critically about Discipline-Based World Wide Web Resources."

4. "Ten C's for Evaluating Internet Resources" http://www.uwec.edu/Admin/Library/Guides/tencs.html. Clear, easy to apply guidelines for assessing Internet sites; link to "Citing Datafiles & Internet Sources" for documentation guidelines.

5. "Evaluating World Wide Web Information" http://crab.rutgers.edu/~scholzcr/eval.html. Guidelines for what and where to look when evaluating Internet sites.

6. "Evaluating Web Resources" http://www-sul.stanford.edu/depts/ssrg/africa/evalu.html. Journal article and extensive bibliography of resources for evaluating information on the Internet.

7. "A Student's Guide to Research with the WWW" http://www.slu.edu/departments/english/research/. A student tutorial on research methods and web site evaluation; includes a bibliography of Internet links to sites on evaluating content, search strategies, and citation style guides.

REFERENCES

Geography for Life: National Geography Standards 1994. (1994) Geography Education Standards Project. Washington, DC: National Geographic Society.

Index

About the Authors

MARTHA B. SHARMA is a Geography teacher at National Cathedral School in Washington, D.C., and an active member of the National Council for Geographic Education. She is the 1999 recipient of the George J. Miller Award for Distinguished Service in Geographic Education.

GARY S. ELBOW is a Professor of Geography at Texas Tech University and an active member in the National Council for Geographic Education. He is author of several geography and social science textbooks.